The Lady of the House

THE LADY
OF
THE HOUSE

The Autobiography of
Sally Stanford

G. P. PUTNAM'S SONS
NEW YORK

Fifth Impression

Library of Congress Catalog
Card Number: 66-14341

To the Real Friends

and not to the tear-in-eye hand-squeezers, nor to the throb-in-throat sweet-talkers, nor to the escape-clause pals, nor to the fee-needing friends, nor to the if, but and providing people is this book dedicated.

Instead, I fondly dedicate this record of memories and accumulated philosophies and mature opinions to the strong and good and loyal companions of my life who were still around when the chips were down, when my back was to the wall, when the breaks were few and the luck was bad. You know who you are and well do I. Someday we will hold a reunion in a good-sized telephone booth.

SALLY STANFORD

The Lady of the House

Prologue

I DIDN'T set out to be a madam any more than Arthur Michael Ramsey, when he was a kid, set out to be Archbishop of Canterbury. Things just happened to both of us, I guess. At a time when most young girls decide to become schoolteachers, actresses, or lady lawyers, one doesn't, after carefully considering all the vocations open to a female, say, "That's for me; I'm going to be a madam." Madaming is the sort of thing that happens to you—like getting a battlefield commission or becoming the Dean of Women at Stanford University. But I have never been the least bit touchy or sensitive about it— never. Many are called, I always say, but few are chosen; and for me it has been a steppingstone to bigger and more profitable things. (I started to say "bigger and better things," but is there really anything better, in the words of the poet, than "living in a house by the side of the road and being a friend to man?")

No, no one sets out to be a madam; but madams answer the call of a well-recognized and very basic human need. Their responsibilities are thrust upon them by the fundamental nitwittedness and economic shortsightedness of most hustling broads. And they become tempered and sharpened and polished to the highest degree of professional awareness by constant intercourse with men devoutly dedicated to the policy of getting something for nothing.

It doesn't take much to produce a good merchant of cash-and-carry love: just courage, an infinite capacity for perpetual suspicion, stamina on a 24-hour-a-day basis, the deathless conviction that the customer is always wrong, a fair knowledge of first and second aid, do-it-yourself gynecology, judo—and a tremendous sense of humor. Aside from these basic talents, a good madam must possess an understanding of female psychology (in the broadest sense), a knowledge of quick therapies for restoring drunks to a state of locomotion (so as to depart the premises), and a grasp of techniques for the eradication of pimps, who are the crabgrass of prostitution. Pimps are always moving in where the green stuff is thickest. With these qualities, and a few others, you may develop into a self-respecting madam. (A good Secretary of State could use some of the same.)

Morality?

As far as I'm concerned, morality is just a word that describes the current fashion of conduct. The Navajo Indians regarded it immoral for old people to live after they could no longer take care of themselves. When aging Navajos could no longer chew their pemmican, they were sent to their Happy Hunting Grounds. We civilized folks keep our elder citizens alive with drugs, intravenous feedings, and surgery, knowing full well we have prolonged only agony and pain.

The immoral Mohammedans can have as many wives as they can properly care for, a caper that our morality doesn't buy. Good old moral Christians like us can have all kinds of husbands or wives, as long as we keep them one at a time, and a good fib in court separates one from the other. Moral America finds itself practicing such noble customs as capital punishment (civil murder) and anti-birth control laws that spawn poverty.

The Lady of the House

Why is the bliss of ignorance considered so moral? My blood pressure goes up and my voltage charges when I realize that more attention is put drilling our young people on dental than on sexual hygiene. Syphilis and gonorrhea could go the way of smallpox and scarlet fever. They could be eradicated in a matter of months, but we stick our moral heads in the sand, sing hymns and say prayers, and cover the stinking problem as a cat buries its dirt.

People ask me what I hate. It's very simple. Phonies, ignorance, and poverty; and not necessarily in that order. I used to think that the primeval curse was the lack of money. Now I've licked that problem. But in my own life I find myself entangled in a jungle of spiritual poverty, intellectual poverty, and the rankest growth of all: the poverty of human kindness and concern about the pain and suffering of other people.

So why should I worry about being immoral in someone's daffy code book merely because . . . once upon a time . . . I permitted a generation of Adams to tarry in my Eden?

When I spoke of madamhood having served as a stepping-stone to bigger things, I was referring to my graduation into rehabilitation and respectability (rehabilitation being used here in the sense of my retirement from the professional life I once knew, and not as a form of repentant apology for something I've always considered a community service). Today, I own and operate one of the best restaurants the West has ever seen—in Sausalito, that beautiful San Francisco suburb. I am one of the Directors of the Sausalito Chamber of Commerce and an officer on its "Ways and Means" committee. Here last year, and for the second time, I ran for a seat on the City Council and damn near made it both times, being defeated only because of a group of local matrons who'd rather have seen Judas Iscariot get the job, provided he was a Republican and would shave. I really consider it a wonderful honor to have received so many votes during those elections, and I will run again and again until I make it . . . if only to hear myself addressed as "Madam Councilman."

Respectability has come to me now, but I have a wonderful storehouse of memories of a full and gratifying life, as well as a damn good income—legitimately. True, I have not been asked as yet to address a girl's graduation class on the subject of the sporting life. But as for *my* life, I wouldn't change a day of it. In truth, I've always regarded my promotion of man's favorite indoor sport as a thoroughly legitimate business and even, as I implied earlier, even a social service. Nobody sent for the customers. They arrived eager to barter and participate in the marketplace of love, and the doors of all my homes as well as my "houses" opened two ways.

As to my claim to performing a useful social service, every lusty, tourist-jammed seaport town like San Francisco needs safety valves and outlets for its males. Shut down a town and the rape rate soars higher than an astronaut while the economy of many a deserving "lady of the evening" drops and no one's really happy except the blue noses.

Mind you, I'm not trying to kid anyone that my journey along the primrose path has made easier for me my roles in life as a restaurateur, lady politician, real estate investor and steadily rising pillar of society. However, it is a fact that I have learned more of human values and of life than I ever would have anywhere else or in any other field; and that includes the ones I worked in as a child.

So how did I become a madam in the first place? You see, it all started in Oregon with a row of goddamn carrots. . . .

One

AS far as I'm concerned, poverty hasn't one redeeming feature
. . . as I found out when I was a child. I was raised—most
kids are "reared," but I was "raised"—on a God-awful, fertile-
as-the-Sahara, close-to-nowhere farm outside of Baker, Oregon.
There was my poor mother, my ineffectual but well-intentioned
father, my three brothers, two sisters and myself—six light-
hearted and raggedy-assed kiddies fighting starvation and poverty in an Oregon gulch.

We were so poor we envied everyone we ever heard of. I
remember my first pangs of guilt and jealousy when I saw the
clothes worn by the minister's daughter. Everyone knows that
the daughters of rural ministers are the worst dressed children
this side of the poorhouse. But *my* minister's daughter wore far
better clothes than *I* ever dreamed of, as well as a pair of shiny
patent leather shoes.

My mother was devoted to her religion, her children, and
respectability, and so she sent us off each Sunday to church with
a coin in our hands for the collection plate. Regardless of
whether or not the nickel she gave me for the minister might
have been needed for a loaf of bread or flour, she was able to say

that she at *least* supported her church. The sermon given by the minister never made tremendous sense to me. My mind was on the nickel in my hand, and logic told me he didn't need the coin as badly as we did.

Down the road was a bakery, where, at the back door on Sunday, I could get two loaves of yesterday's bread for my nickel. So I did. I didn't dare tell how the bread got into the house. I just put it there and said nothing. Mother said, "The Lord will Provide," but I was thinking about the shiny patent leather shoes the minister's daughter wore.

When I was seven years old, they built a golf clubhouse, quite a rare event in Baker, Oregon. The boys around town talked about something they called "caddies" and about how much money could be made by carrying around the players' clubs. So I went to the golf course and sat up on the benches to see what was going on. I got the drift of the game in time, and I got the drift that the men who were swinging the clubs at those little white balls had money. One day as I sat on the bench watching intently, one of the players came up to me and asked, "Hey kid, do you want to be a caddy?" Apparently he couldn't find any of the boys around, but I was eager to learn and earn, so I said "Sure." The S.O.B. made me carry his golf bag around all day. Not only *his*, but some other jerk's as well.

The going rate was fifteen cents a round, and I went around and around and around. At the end of the day I was absolutely dead on my feet, but the dollar and a half he gave me somehow seemed to dull the pains a little. They asked me if I wanted to come back the next day and do it again (a question I've been asked often since) and again I said "Sure."

My mother wasn't exactly happy about my being around all those men, but that dollar and a half turned the tide. My father was ecstatic. I kept the job seven days a week—every day after school and weekends between 7 A.M. and the onset of darkness.

The Lady of the House

Around dusk all the players would go to the "19th hole" and get loaded while I took my hard-earned dollars home and delivered every penny to my mother. As I look back, I remember the great thrill of seeing her face when I gave it to her, and it kind of made it all worthwhile to me. Almost.

Besides having to hold down my responsibilities in this new rich man's sport of golf, I still had to tend to my other work around the house and keep trying to outwit my older sister. She had taken it upon herself to be my personal watchdog, for every once in a while even a little money-maker like me had to take a break.

Once, when I was eight years old, I took it into my head that I wanted a penny for a piece of candy or two. At that time my earnings at the golf course were getting to be pretty damn good but I never saved any for myself. So I "borrowed" a penny from my mother's purse when she went outside. At least I *thought* it was a penny. It was about the same size, although a slightly different color and little bit shinier. It turned out to be a five-dollar gold piece. The last five dollars in the whole damn house. Still thinking it was a penny, I took it to the general store, which carried everything from a threshing machine to pins. I gave the merchant the coin and he helped me to select what I wanted. He'd been taking advantage of me for a long time obviously, because I *never* had a penny with the buying power of the one I'd just given him.

When I left the store I had two big bags full of two-for-a-penny and three-for-a-penny candy and considered myself to be one hell of a barterer. I invited every friend (and stranger) my age, including my watchdog sister, and we hid under the boardwalk and had the biggest sweets feast you've ever seen. We ate and ate until the stuff came out of our ears and then I hid the half bag or so that remained, that we couldn't quite shove down, and went home. My mother discovered the loss of the gold piece and quizzed us kids about it. Hell, I hadn't seen any five-dollar gold piece (and I wouldn't know one if I did). All *I* took was a penny, so I said "No ma'am."

When Mother asked my big sister she said, "Marcy (Marcia being my given name) knows . . . Marcy knows." (The fink.) Finally the story came out and Mother went to the general store, found out about the five dollars' worth of candy and nearly blew the place off the map. I went back to the hiding place to get the candy that was left, and the bag was gone. I still think my sister filched it.

Golf balls in those days used to cost as much as four and five dollars apiece, but most of the players never bothered to tip you if you recovered one that they had lost. Because of their value at the time, each player usually carved or stamped his initials on them for identification. Still plenty got lost, and when I wasn't working at caddying, I used to look for the little lost spheres. In time I developed a hell of a collection, for somehow the initials on them became blurred.

One day, while I waited on the first tee for a client who was getting stiff in the clubhouse, I took one of his precious golf balls and his driver and, just for fun, I swacked the ball with everything I had toward the first hole green. The head of the club hit the ball perfectly and, with a sound like the report of a pistol, that ball shot out into space and straight down the fairway. It was a beautiful shot, but I didn't mean to hit it so *hard*. Now I had to get the damn ball back before my customer came out. I raced down the range toward the first green looking everywhere I went. I thought I'd seen it hit the green but when I got there it was nowhere to be found. I was getting worried and as a last desperate chance I halfheartedly glanced into the cup. Lo and behold! A little ball was staring up at me. I took it from the cup and sure as hell, it belonged to my client. What an experience that was. I was both thrilled at my feat and relieved at finding the ball at all. So, without a witness anywhere to share my glory, I shot a hole-in-one right there in Baker, Oregon, at the age of eight. But the scare I had when I thought I had lost his precious ball taught me once and for all to play with nobody's balls but my own.

Somewhere around my ninth birthday, a customer I caddied for quite frequently asked me what I wanted for my birthday. His merely *asking* was rare enough, but when I told him my heart's desire was a pair of Mary Jane patent leather shoes with a strap across the front and a button on the sides, he did something even rarer. He pulled two real silver dollars from his pocket and handed them to me. "Go ahead and buy yourself a pair," he said. His giving me those two dollars was the most fantastic thing that ever had happened to me, and I ran right home to tell my mother.

I think perhaps she had other ideas for the money, but it would have taken the state militia and an Act of Congress to make me even *consider* using that money for anything else but a pair of Mary Janes. So Mother and I went downtown to the Golden Rule Department Store on Main Street. The owner was a real merchandiser and I remember acres and acres of brightly colored and fancifully displayed items—every one of which I wanted. But those Mary Jane shoes were my main objective that day even though, in the back of my mind, there existed another item. Hair ribbons. The Mary Janes would cost all of the two dollars and so I wouldn't have money enough for the ribbons too, but it certainly would be nice if I could have both. The only thing my sisters and I had to tie our long, chestnut-brown hair up with were rubber bands, and we were damn lucky to have them. I had often considered filching some from the Christmas decorations box in the closet at home where my sister and I would go periodically to tear off a small piece of red crepe paper which we would wet and rub on our lips, rouge being far beyond our economic or moral reach.

While Mother kept trying to steer me toward those morbid black and brown utility shoes with the metal taps on the toes for longer wear, my eyes kept wandering to the ribbon counter. At last I stood transfixed in front of it, my eyes glued to the miles and miles of breathtakingly beautiful colors. Suddenly, I felt eyes on me and I looked to my side and lifted my head and there was the most elegant lady I had ever seen. She had a frilly laced front white silk blouse covered by a small sealskin black jacket. On her head was perched an elaborate black velvet hat with great black ostrich feathers which hung dramatically over one side. She smiled down on me sympathetically, probably thinking "Poor waif," and started to talk to me about the ribbons. Suddenly, my arm was jerked from behind and my mother dragged me back to the shoe department, muttering that we couldn't afford the ribbons and that I mustn't talk to strange ladies.

Mother tried vainly to convince me to buy another pair of utility shoes but I won out, and she went over to the salesgirl to negotiate the sale. I stole quickly and quietly back to the ribbon counter to do a little negotiating of my own. The beautiful lady was still there and when she saw me once again looking longingly in front of the counter, she bent down slightly and asked, "Would you like to have some of those hair ribbons, little girl?" Would I like some hair ribbons! Is a pig's behind pork? I nodded as demurely as I could and she gave some sort of an order to the salesgirl behind the counter. I watched with envy as she unwound yards and yards of every type of hair ribbon, in every color as well. I thought it was all for my newfound friend, but it wasn't. It was all for *me*. Before I could swoon with joy, the tall attractive lady took the bag from the clerk and laid it on the counter in front of me, winking knowingly and smiling sweetly as she walked away. I got the message, *and* the hair ribbons. I took the bag from the counter, stuffed it under my jacket and joined my mother.

My mother had often told me not to talk to strangers but she had seemed to be especially adamant about the lady in the ribbon department. When we got home, and after I had hidden the ribbons in my room, I asked my mother, "Momma . . . why didn't you want me to talk to that nice lady?"

"No, Marcy," she said as she busied herself with other things. "You know you are not supposed to talk to strangers."

"But," I explained, "she was such a *nice* lady."

"She was not a nice lady," my mother said finally, "she was a *painted* lady and I don't want you to ever talk to her again."

A "painted" lady? Hell, she didn't look painted to me. True, she was wearing real rouge on her face and her eyebrows were darker than Mother's, but she sure as hell didn't look painted. Besides, she was damn nice to me. So I kept my secret and the ribbons to myself for about two months and then one day I came home from the golf course and told my mother that the wife of one of the club members had given me all those beautiful ribbons. She believed me, or at least accepted my story rather than believe worse, and I was able to wear them everywhere, in front of God and everybody. It was marvelous.

My new shiny patent leather shoes were shown off proudly on the golf links the very next day. Probably the only thing that detracted from my new "image" of prosperity was my bending over to pick up golf balls in full view of my customers, which enabled them to see my bloomers. That was socially acceptable for a girl of my young years, but the problem was the non-paid advertisement that stretched across the seat, reading HAPPY VALLEY FLOUR.

In my mother's attempts at making something out of nothing (and she really was a clever gal) she fashioned rather undainty underthings out of the strongest and easiest-to-acquire materials available. Namely, "Happy Valley" flour sacks. And not only did she create brightly colored underthings for us kids, but she extended her genius to "Happy Valley" flour sack curtains and "Happy Valley" flour sack patchwork quilts, aprons and dish towels. I've often wished that I could find some material as strong as "Happy Valley" sacks and some dye as indelible. You could *never* get rid of it.

Emily was one of my dearest friends and was multipurposeful by virtue of being a chicken, which allowed me to make a few more dollars for the family (in my usual Robin Hood fashion) during my spare time away from caddying.

I had taken fourteen eggs (Plymouth Rock variety) and placed them under the warm and dedicated supervision of Emily (also of Plymouth Rock lineage). She hatched eleven of the fourteen, but unfortunately one died right after birth. The remaining ten managed to grow up to a youthful age, with my help and some corn and wheat feed, which makes for nice fat chickens.

One day my mother commented on the fact that the chickens I had raised were reaching the fryer age. This didn't bother me too much as I owed allegiance only to Emily and on a farm you have to learn to understand these things. However, I had been down to the butcher shop in Baker and overheard the butcher mention to a customer that he was buying frying chickens for seventy-five cents a piece. Now that was a hell of a lot of money for just a chicken.

I knew that my mother planned to kill them and cook them one by one for the family, but that seventy-five cents a chicken stuck in my head and I thought of the wonderful things I could buy for the house and family with that kind of money. So I devised a plan of action.

The Lady of the House

I started by taking one of the chickens and carried it lovingly in my arms to the butcher shop, feeling like a baby kidnapper and also a murderer of sorts. The butcher grabbed the young pullet roughly by the legs and threw her on the scale to weigh her. When I saw how he was handling the poor thing I almost changed my mind, but she was going to "get it in the neck," as they say, whether at the butcher shop or at home, and there *was* that matter of six bits.

Part of my plan called for me to explain to the butcher that I had to have the head and the feet for the dogs and cats on the farm and I said, "And the feathers, I'll have to have them too. My mother wants to make feather pillows with them." He looked at me rather oddly, but since I would have it no other way and since he didn't need those portions, he gave them to me.

So with seventy-five cents in one hand and one of Emily's daughter's head, feet and feathers in the other, I made it back to the farm. I carefully, and without being seen, strewed the feathers around an area of the chicken yard. I laid out the two feet and the head (stepping on it a little to cover up the clean cut in the neck) and waited for my mother to discover the crime.

"Do you think the dog did it?" she asked, as she stood over the remains of Emily's child. Our dog, a beautiful Irish setter, wouldn't have hurt a chicken for the world. But he was a suspect. My mother carefully inspected his jaws for any telltale signs of pin feathers and, finding none, released him from custody.

"Weasels!" she finally said. "It must be weasels."

Now the groundwork had been laid, and one by one I abducted the chickens until there were only about four or five left. By this time the weasel theory was wearing kind of thin. My mother ran the gamut of possibilities from foxes to badgers, until one slight complication set in. My sharp-eyed mother caught on to the fact that the feet were cleanly cut off.

"Now, what kind of an animal could do that?" she asked of my father. He volunteered a few species of wildlife, but I knew that the situation was getting a little warm.

To compensate, I informed the butcher that from now on he would only have to give me the head of the chicken. That was the only part that went over well with my mother so I figured I'd eliminate the rest of the evidence. The money I spent on the way home each night from the golf course to buy something for the house or the family. It was a worthwhile, though devious, method of getting something else into the house besides empty liquor bottles and colds.

The only trouble with Baker was that my father was not only an indifferent farmer, he was also an indifferent gambler and a frequent drinker. If everything didn't go just his way, he'd chuck the whole works and leave it all, headed for new and what he wanted to believe were "greener" pastures.

Behind us in our pastoral paupery in rural Oregon was a history of domestic, social and economic flops. My mother was a schoolteacher and had homesteaded three hundred and sixty acres of land in Burnt River, Oregon, close to Baker, before she married my father. He had done the same and, by coincidence, his three hundred and sixty were right next door to hers. She worked her land and was getting it somewhere. He received just compensation for his efforts too, which amounted to slightly less than nothing. However, painting a beautiful picture of wedded and financial bliss, he convinced my mother to marry him in Holy Wedlock—and landlock—which rapidly developed into a deadlock and they jointly lost the whole bundle.

It took my father four years finally to lose everything in Burnt River and with my older sister Juanita in tow, they bought a house on one acre of land on a corner across from the golf links in Baker. Baker lasted longer than most other homesteads, and two more children, myself and my brother Art, were born there. We were the total crop raised by my father during that period. His odd jobs here and there helped my mother and myself pay off some of the mortgage he had little by little created on the property.

So, having accomplished the creation of three children and little else, my father once again moved, after ten years in Baker, to find his greener pastures. The place was called Sunnyslope, Oregon, about five miles outside of Baker on the old Oregon Trail, and I left my highly profitable caddying job at the golf club and all my friends. Sunnyslope was, I have to admit, sunny. But we "sloped" right down toward foreclosure from the first day we stepped onto the premises. However, in Sunnyslope I received several other lessons in living and valuable facts of life.

Least of importance to you, but extremely valuable to me at the time, was a partial renewal in my faith in Santa Claus, when, for Christmas at Sunnyslope, I received the most beautiful doll in the world. It had been made by my mother out of one of two china heads of dolls that belonged to my grandmother when she was a child. My sister got one and I got one and they were beautiful. (Though naturally, mine was the prettier.) Her body was made out of a pair of old jeans stuffed with sawdust. I named her "Pansy." I loved her very dearly, but, like most children, she had an aversion to being washed. And, unlike most children, she mildewed. Each time the mildew broke through the material, I had to wash her off, and dry her before she mildewed again. Somehow she never quite dried out before the mildew appeared.

She had black hair and blue eyes and she was beautiful, but one day she unexpectedly came up with a fractured skull; more specifically, my dear father became angry at my spending too much time in the playhouse and kicked Pansy right square in the head. She was never the same, but I keep her still, broken head and all. After all, she *was* my daughter.

For several months my mother had been getting fat. "Fat," she quickly pointed out to me was not a nice word. I could use the word "stout" or "heavy" but not "fat." She was an English teacher so I figured she knew what she was saying. But it did seem to me that she was getting awfully fat.

Finally one day she sent my sister and me out of the house and told us to play up the road with some neighbors about a mile away. I didn't want to go, and I couldn't figure why she wanted us to play with *those* kids anyhow. She'd never seemed to like them. They were no poorer than we, but they couldn't keep themselves clean. Rich we were not, but clean we were.

Despite my protests, my sister and I did as we were told. Once I got there, though, we started to fight, and I had just decided that I was going to go back home whether my mother said to or not, when a big, red, shiny automobile drove by. Well, this was a rare sight indeed in that country. *Any* car would have caused a stir, but *this* was the most beautiful car in the world. I stood transfixed for a few minutes watching it until it was out of sight around the bend.

My sister tried to stop me, but I ran up the road and hid in the thickest part of the brush until she gave up looking for me. Then, I started the long walk home.

When I got to the front of the house, lo and behold, there was that shiny red car. Its seats were black leather, all tufted, and it was truly lovely. I ran to the front porch to find out who owned it and my father caught me at the screen door, a big smile on his ruddy face, and he said, "Marcy, I've got a big surprise for you."

"What is it?" I said. "A hair ribbon?"

"No, not that," he said.

The Lady of the House

"A pair of shoes?" I asked again.

"No."

"Maybe a doll," I hoped.

"No . . . no."

There was only one hope left and the only thing I really wanted right then. Especially after that walk home in the dry and dusty heat.

"Is it a watermelon?" I beamed.

"No, Marcy. You have to go in and ask your mother."

Dutifully I went inside and looked for my mother. In the living room were two strangers, a man and a woman.

"Where's Momma?" I said.

The strange man in the dark suit told me that I could go in and see my mother, so I went into the bedroom and found her in bed. Tears in my eyes (because I thought she must be sick), I kissed her on the cheek and sat down in the rocking chair by her side.

The room suddenly filled with the damnedest din you've ever heard. Everyone was lunging toward me, and my mother and the strange woman screamed, "The baby . . . the baby . . . you're sitting on the baby."

Well, I'll be damned. It *was* a baby. I stood by the rocking chair and looked down at that tiny little thing and thought to myself, It's the same size as Pansy. How wonderful.

My father said, "You have a new baby brother, Marcy."

I thought, He'll be a *lot* more fun than Pansy.

Besides, Pansy had a broken head.

I was thrilled to death and I turned toward my mother and said, "Where did he come from?"

She pulled me toward the bed and explained that the stork had brought him and it had ridden up to the house perched on the back of the doctor's car. Well, that proved to me that the strange man in the black suit was a doctor, but I sure as hell wasn't going to fall for that bit about a stork perched on the back of the car.

"Oh, no," I said. "I saw the car drive up the road and I didn't see any stork."

With a little thinking, she finally worked her way around to explaining that the stork had sat crouched down low in the front seat next to the doctor so that the wind wouldn't hit it.

Well, that was better. Just one minor flaw remained.

"Well, then, what happened to the stork?"

"Well," my mother explained, "he had so many other things to do he flew away just before you came."

Which cleared the air completely. Full of my newfound knowledge and my new brother, I ran next door to my two girl friends and we went to the dollhouse where I gave them the great news.

I explained in vivid detail about the stork and everything Mother had told me, and even went so far as to say I'd *seen* the bird when the car went by. My girl friends laughed out loud and said, "You don't believe that stuff, do you?"

Hell yes, I believed it. Not only did I believe it, but I was willing to fight to the death to defend every word.

So the two sisters spent about an hour telling me all about having a baby, and even all about *not* having one. Keee-rist. They described all the details. It was absolutely absurd. My mother would *definitely* not do anything like *that*, ever. I wasn't so sure of my father, but I defended him anyhow. To cap off their biology lesson, one of the girls said, "And besides, before you can have a baby, you have to ----" and that infamous four-letter word hit my tender ears for the first time. They not only said the word, but they spelled it out for me and explained the full impact of its meaning.

This was the damnedest piece of news I had ever heard. I decided to keep quiet about it and see if I couldn't detect something suspicious going on between my mother and father. I didn't. But the word stuck in my head. I said it over and over again in my mind and wondered if I shouldn't just ask Mother what it meant and get it over with.

Unfortunately, I picked the worst time in the world to ask the question. It was a Sunday afternoon and all our relatives in the area had shown up for the traditional Sunday dinner. During one of those lulls in conversation, I decided to make my move.

"Mommy," I said in my high-pitched voice, "what does - - - - mean?" I not only said the word, but I spelled it out too. There was a pregnant pause. Then my mother yelled across the table, "*What* did you say?"

Well, she *asked*, and so I repeated it, including the spelling.

My father practically had a coronary and Mother was speechless. I was never moved so fast from any one spot in my life. My father swept me off my chair and carried me (or threw me, I can't remember which) into the kitchen. The kitchen was the place you always went preparatory to the woodshed.

It was pretty obvious that I had messed up somewhere, and a well-placed whipping was the only answer I got.

At the tender age of nine I became too elderly and too well educated for any further extravagance in the direction of higher education—after all, I'd made it through the third grade. I was put to work in a truck garden. In fact, I was put in charge of the whole operation. I broke-up and prepared the soil as soon as the snow melted in the spring, planted the seeds, irrigated the land by hand, harvested it, then loaded the stuff into a big cart which my mother and I would push five miles into town. There we peddled from door to door.

To this day, every time I hear the swish-hipped bucolic types in *Oklahoma* singing estatically about the joys of farm life, I could hit Rodgers with Hammerstein. Agriculture is very well for farmers and composers, but not for little girls who'd rather be playing with dolls.

Then, once more, my wandering father got the bug and we moved. This time, at the age of eleven, I found myself in Victorville, California, down by Barstow on the edge of the Mojave Desert. The only thing my father could have ever raised on land like that was a perpetual thirst, which he did with great success. He had placed a down-payment on a piece of property but never went near it except to sleep. His odd jobs in town and my ironing shirts at "twelve-for-a-half-a-buck" paid the mortgage for awhile. I didn't mind the ironing so much, it was waiting for the fifty cents that got *me*.

This miserable period of my life lasted for two hot, humid years before my father finally decided to move again. This time it was to the metropolis of Medford, Oregon. Shortly after arriving, and by pure luck, I was able to get a job as a housekeeper and do-it-all, which included cleaning house, lawn and garden, and tending anything else necessary, for the family that owned the Golden Rule Department Store chain. My salary was three dollars a week. Mother took in laundry, and Father worked hard at staying out of work. At *that* he was a professional.

Just before leaving Victorville, I had been given a small dog— a combination of Pekingese and Pomeranian with a little French poodle thrown in just for fun. To me she was beautiful, and I named her "Daphne." I carried her on the train to Medford, with my mother and brothers and sisters, in the bosom of my dress so as to avoid having to pay fare for her.

One day in Medford I came home and Daphne was mysteriously missing. I looked everywhere for her until finally someone told me that a woman who owned the candy store in town had a dog that looked like my Daphne. My legs moving as fast as they could, I went to the store and asked the woman if she'd seen my little dog. She had. In fact, she *owned* it. My mother had sold

Daphne to the lady for five dollars. I begged her and pleaded, offering to work for a whole year for nothing if she'd just give Daphne back to me. But my tears and my pleading had no effect. I'll never forget that woman. Heavyset, with hard eyes and heavy jowls. Her eyeglasses hung around her bulbous neck from thin chains attached to the stems.

Crying all the way, I went home and faced my mother.

"Daphne, Momma. Why did you sell Daphne?"

My mother's face was sad.

"Oh, honey," she said, her hands taking me by my shoulders, "I *didn't* want to sell your dog. Marcy, you love your brothers and sisters, don't you?"

"Yes," I said, not understanding her logic. "But why did you sell my dog?"

Mother sighed. "Marcy . . . we have no food in the house. We couldn't afford to *care* for Daphne the way we should. I needed that money, Marcy, for food, for the family. Do you understand? We'll get you another dog, honey . . . just as soon as we can afford one. Just you wait and see."

For months I hounded that candy store woman, trying to see Daphne, pleading for her to let me have her back. She kept Daphne out of sight and I could only see her from a distance sometimes as I came into town, before she'd pick Daphne up and take her inside.

To take my mind off Daphne, I worked all the harder at keeping house for the owners of the Golden Rule. (Something they never personally followed themselves. They had changed it to read "Do unto others, before they do you.") Then one payday, as some women do when they feel down in the dumps, I wandered downtown on my way home to look in the store windows. I had my three dollars and I had the misfortune of passing the local emporium of high fashion. There in the window was the most gorgeous, soul-satisfying pair of high-button, high-heeled, black and white shoes, on sale for $1.68. I really had no intentions of buying anything, but I just *had* to try them on. God, they were magnificent. They changed my whole life. The clerk suggested I buy a pair of white lisle stockings at forty-seven cents a pair. With both the stockings and the shoes, and a free buttonhook thrown in, I succumbed.

With my new finery I marched, ecstatic with pride, to the largest building in town, the local railroad station, which housed the only Chinese café in town, and ordered a shrimp salad. Each night when I worked in the home of the Golden Rule owners, they served shrimp salad; and each night I had to wash the damn dishes without one bit of it left for me.

The Chinese owner, chef, maître d', waiter and dishwasher, asked me if I would like to have a cup of coffee to go with the salad. Naturally I said yes. Would I like some bread and butter? "Of course." And how about a piece of lemon chiffon pie? "Well, yes."

I was just finishing the pie when I heard the irate voice of my father, who was accompanied by the local constable. Not only was I late home by some hours but I was in debt to the café owner, and Father wanted me to return the shoes and get that money back. But the store and I were in agreement. We both refused to take back the shoes. Father was furious. He and the constable were drinking chums, and my spree had spoiled their plans. The constable, a huge man with a walruslike mustache, frightened me thoroughly. Some months later when he was found face down in Bear Creek, I felt no great sorrow. He was my first brush with the law.

Two

THEN came the news of the simultaneous deaths of two of my young aunts in Peru, California. They'd been on vacation, staying in a fishing lodge, when a great oil field fire broke out and killed them and quite a few others before they could escape.

That was October 2, 1917. A brood of small cousins were left motherless at their homes in Santa Paula, and I was summoned by my grandparents and my Uncle Peter to come down and help out as best I could. They say that an "ill wind brings no good," but this one probably saved me from becoming a farm animal in long skirts, and I quickly prepared to leave.

Santa Paula, California, wasn't exactly Paris, but it was all new to me, and I was able to wear a dress, put up my hair, and roll up my stockings—all pretty big stuff. Being the new girl in town, I soon came to the attention of a young oil field worker named LeRoy Snyder. His sister was also lost in the fire in Peru, and so it was inevitable that we'd meet.

LeRoy was a tall, good-looking kid with an easygoing personality and a typically rural background. He tried very hard to make me like him, and he succeeded—as much as a young man can with a girl fourteen and a half years old. After a respectable period of courting, he asked me to marry him. The excitement of the proposal, plus the possibility of my never having to return to Medford, was a hard combination to beat. Besides, at that time in my life, matrimony looked pretty damn good to me. I figured it would be an easy way to get out of housework and gardening and those damn carrots. I think I would have married a Kodiak bear, provided it was a male and fairly clean.

We painted some pretty attractive pictures in our minds of our married life together and decided to go through with it. We took his mother's car and drove to Ventura where the marriage laws were less stringent. I told the county clerk I was eighteen and LeRoy said he was twenty-one. He was nineteen. Then we found a justice of the peace and I heard those fateful words for the first of what would be several times. LeRoy suddenly became my husband, to have and to hold, in sickness and in health, for about nine hours.

After the simple (but effective) wedding ceremony, we drove back to his mother's home in Santa Paula. On the way I remember telling LeRoy that now I was married, I wanted to do something-or-other. He said, "Oh, no. You can't do that. You're *mine* now." I don't remember what it was that I wanted to do, but I *do* remember that I didn't appreciate him telling me I was "his" so damn finally. I had made up my mind that I wasn't going to "belong" to *anyone*.

LeRoy's mother tried very hard to make our wedding night memorable, but it soon became "memorable" on its own merits. After a sumptuous wedding feast of shrimp salad, chili con carne and watermelon, we retired to our room upstairs. LeRoy went down the hall for a few moments (too few) and returned dressed in a new pair of store-creased cerise pajamas and the kind of look on his face that hogs have when the trough is full. I was still wearing my blue organdy, my total trousseau along with my spare combination and my toothbrush, and was sitting on the edge of the bed with my hands in my lap, wondering "What's next?"

Drooling ever so slightly, LeRoy suggested that I take off my organdy and put it over the back of the chair in the corner.

"What for?" I asked in amazement.

He looked at me rather curiously, wiped his hand over his mouth and asked, "Well, then, would you at least like to take off your shoes?"

Being quite comfortable the way I was, I again asked "What for?"

LeRoy let out a little sigh, pulled the chair closer to the bed, sat on it, and began to give me the answer to my question. He talked on and on until the whole picture took shape in my mind. I couldn't believe my ears.

I couldn't believe that *anyone*, outside of the French whom I'd heard would do anything, could bring themselves to do what LeRoy described. I was scared out of my wits.

There is a time for talk and a time for action. Poor LeRoy talked too damn much. Before he could act on his unthinkable plans, I vaulted the bed, ran down the stairs and out of his mother's house with all possible speed. Stopping to thank her for her hospitality never entered my mind. I left behind me forever my curlers, my underwear, my toothbrush and big-mouthed LeRoy.

Fortunately, I had a five-dollar bill with me and so I ran downtown to the Pickwick Stage (forerunner of our Greyhound buses) and asked how much a ticket to Medford, Oregon, would be. I was just a little over thirty dollars short. I sat in the station for a long time, crying softly, trying to figure out what in hell I was going to do *now*. I didn't have any intentions of going back to that sex fiend LeRoy, and I knew that my grandparents, my uncle, LeRoy and his mother would all be looking for me.

The answer to my problem came in the form of a retired army sergeant, about forty-five years old, who saw me crying and offered his help. I told him that I wanted to go home to Medford, Oregon, because my mother was sick.

To make a long story short, this nice guy pushed up a trip he was going to make a week later to Portland, Oregon, and offered me a ride in his car all the way. Naturally I went. If there were any strings attached in his mind, I wouldn't have known about them anyway, and he acted like the perfect gentlemen that he was. Two days later I was back in Medford.

When I stood in front of my parents' home I felt as though I were falling back into a well it had taken me years to climb out of. I wondered if I'd ever get out again.

My father, of course, was tickled almost sober when he saw he had his little worker back to help pay the rent, but Mother was worried about my happiness. Personally, I felt that Medford, and even my father, were better than what LeRoy had planned for me.

The weeks went by and LeRoy sent letter upon letter full of tearfully corny sentiments. He was a sweet guy, as I look back on it all, and if he had spent more time "doing" instead of just "describing," things might have turned out differently. Finally, LeRoy pulled up his nuptial stakes, got an annulment and tossed his dreams about me out the window. Maybe next time he'd lock the door first.

Back in Medford, jobs were harder than hell to get and everyone in town was either eating high on the hog or chewing on its bones. There wasn't any middle class in Medford. I took a job as a waitress at Wong's Café on the main street. Mother didn't like the idea at all, but that's where the money was and so that's where I *had* to be.

The Lady of the House

Day after day I met young men and old men, all of them smiling at me and making passes of one degree or another. I was beginning to see that I had a little more going for me than I had previously thought. Dolls had long ago lost their excitement and I became more interested in the men around me and a little more exciting life (if that was possible in Medford).

The few men I *did* date never found out where I really lived. I had them drop me off in front of one of the attractive homes across town; then I'd walk back across the community of Medford in the middle of the night to my little shack by the tracks.

One of the men I met at Wong's was a good-looking guy much older than I, named Dan Goodan. One evening my mother dropped by the café to see me and met him there. That night, when I arrived home a little later than usual, she asked me if I had been seeing him. I told her no, understanding her tone of voice, and she said, "I'm glad, Marcy; I don't like his looks. I just don't like him."

I wish I had been as astute as my mother. Dan and I dated in secrecy many times, and he talked constantly of how much he loved me and wanted to marry me. More than once (in the heat of the moment) his hands would wander and I thought he was trying to adjust my garters—something I could do very well myself without his help. When he did, I'd push him away and he'd let out with a laugh much like Doug Fairbanks.

Finally Wong's Café, my father, Medford, and everyone in it got on my nerves, and Dan became my sole opportunity for escape. One evening I packed my straw suitcase with three jars of homemade strawberry jam and crept away from the house to meet Dan in town. We would be married, move to his hometown in Colorado and live happily ever after. Where LeRoy talked, Dan acted, and I blissfully surrendered everything but my three jars of strawberry jam before I realized that we'd forgotten something. A little thing called "getting married." Dan laughed like Doug Fairbanks again and said we would tie the knot in Colorado.

Dan was generous to a fault. He asked me if I wanted anything for the journey, and I wanted more than anything else in the world an American Beauty Quick Heating Electric Iron, the most wonderful scientific development of the age. I bought one with a ten-dollar check Dan gave me from the company he worked for, the Weiss Lumber Company of Medford. He was an auditor there and was the grandson of a former governor of Colorado. With this background and his amazing generosity, I figured I'd made a damn good catch.

Our next stop was Eaton, Colorado, Dan's hometown. We got the cottage; we bought new furniture and clothes, and a framed motto which read *Happy is the home where virtue dwells*. Dan paid for all of these things with money from the liberal check he had gotten from the Weiss Lumber Company. The only problem was that the company didn't know a damn thing about it.

One day, shortly after I had decided where to put the new sofa, the police came and collected Dan. It looked like the honeymoon was over.

A couple of days later, when they collected me, I knew damn well it was over, for it was with the Weiss Lumber Company's money that I had purchased the American Beauty Quick Heating Electric Iron. For the second time in my life, I met a policeman non-socially. I've met several since and I know how to handle them now. There are really only three kinds of cops: the nice ones, the hungry ones, and the vicious ones, and sometimes we all get a little hungry, civic bounty for public servants being what it is. Hunger gets us all at times. (Does it surprise you that I am always for increasing policemen's salaries when the subject comes up on the ballot?)

But back there in Eaton, Colorado, I was just a scared teen-aged girl two weeks away from the carrot patch, and I had no defense.

The police sergeant was determined to wring a confession from me. He wanted me to plead guilty, and I said, "No, I won't do it. . . . I didn't do anything and I'm not going to do it." So the Court appointed an attorney, and the D.A. said to Dan and me, "If you don't cost the County a trial, we'll see that you get probation."

After a lot of discussion, and not having a dollar in the world, we did as the D.A. advised. Trusting him was my first mistake. In July of that year I was sentenced to the Oregon State Penitentiary at Salem for two years for obtaining goods under false pretenses. Said goods: one lousy American Beauty Quick Heating Electric Iron.

At that time there were no female prisoners at the Oregon State Penitentiary in Salem and so there were no female matrons. When my guard, who was a woman from Jackson, the county seat, deputized to take me to Salem, brought me before the warden, he took one look at me and screamed, "This isn't any goddamn nursery school. I've got no place for a child like this. That damn judge must be out of his mind."

I started to weep lustily, and the warden ordered me out of the prison at once. The female deputy, who had the heart of a dead mackerel, and several physical similarities, took me in tow and we stayed at the best hotel in town. We stayed until the correctional authorities made it clear that, child or not, society's debt for that damned iron had to be paid, and *not* in Salem's best hotel.

A place was made for me in the Penitentiary and I was given a mountain of sewing to do and for recreation, a little cooking. I remember looking into the mirror every day and saying to myself, "A man got you into this, you dope, and from now on, don't take men seriously. . . . Just 'take' them!"

The Lady of the House

It was there I also made up my mind never to be broke again. Poverty and want and bad luck had snapped at my heels all my life. It seemed that only the poor were punished and the broke went to jail. Do you wonder at my sincere agreement with Prison Warden Duffy, years later, when he made the statement: "The rich are never executed by the State"?

I had just passed eighteen when I came out of prison. The State supplied me with mustering-out pay—"Gate Money" they called it, amounting to five whole dollars. They also supplied me with a job. All outgoing prisoners have to have one of those. It was doing housework from 7 A.M. until 9 P.M. every day for ten dollars a month in Salem, Oregon. All this, they figured, added up to my complete rehabilitation.

When I arrived at the home of my new employer, all her creepy friends were available to take a peek at and hear the scandal of the girl she had so generously taken out of prison. One thing I can say is that she got a damn good worker for next to nothing, the cheapskate.

I had an Uncle Peter in Santa Paula, California, and after my parole was finished and I had been so completely straightened out, I left my fruitful employment with a ticket paid for by Uncle Peter. In Santa Paula I got a job as a waitress in the Pearl Café and met another charming man who was going to show me the way to promotion and pay. But I had already been promoted and had paid for it, so I was out to do a little taking on my own. I'd met a few girls in Salem who told me about the money they had made in the bootlegging business. I was young, good-looking, all 105 pounds of me, and decided to start out on my own.

I never touched a drop of liquor or smoked a cigarette until I was forty-six years of age. After all, I was determined to make money and keep myself virtuous in *some* departments.

The Lady of the House

Business was good and I moved out of my upstairs flat over a chili joint and took a beautiful old Spanish house on a palisade overlooking the Pacific Ocean. I ran a strictly one-woman business, with no confidante, no girl friend, no boy friend, and no one to split the profits with. I had learned early the truth that three people can keep a secret only when two of them die young. And selling illicit liquor to the legitimately thirsty—this had to be top secret.

I did everything myself. I bought my merchandise, paid cash for it, took it home, and personally processed it in the bathtub. A lot of jokes have been made about bathtub gin, but there never was a container more convenient for the production of high-class hooch. In an emergency, the plug could be pulled and all the evidence was far out to sea. Of course, care had to be taken not to leave any of the product in the tub between batches; you could get the damnedest blisters if you were careless.

Five gallons of alcohol cost twenty-five dollars. This had to be cut, flavored with bourbon extract, colored with caramel, bottled and labeled, then aged. I used to age mine about forty-eight hours.

I wasn't enough of a chemist to produce good gin. It was almost as cheap as Clorox at the time and far tastier, so I bought it ready-made. Gordon's was the most popular brand. It sold better than High and Dry. This was a continual mystery to me, since they both came out of the same can and went to the customer undoctored. My customers were just a lot of nice guys from the region with barely enough left over from the necessities of life, like booze, to pay for the luxuries, like bread, potatoes, and shoes. I bought my raw materials from a place called The Rincon, which was very popular with people in my business. The popularity was because the county line ran right through the middle of the house and was so marked. When the

Santa Barbara County Police arrived, we all rushed to the Ventura side of the house and thus couldn't be pinched. It was vice versa when the Ventura County cops dropped by.

You just couldn't take a tumble in this place unless both county policemen arrived at the same time, and somehow this simultaneous action never occurred to them. So I quenched thirsts, made a few dollars for myself, avoided romance, and sublimated my desires by reading good books. I read everything I could get my hands on and spent considerable evenings with Havelock Ellis (there's a card) and Elinor Glyn, and what she doesn't know about sex could be stored in the Grand Canyon with some left over. Some of my favorites: Shakespeare, Dickens, O'Henry, Sinclair Lewis, Somerset Maugham, Jack London, Omar Khayyam, Krafft-Ebing who wrote *Psychopathia Sexualis*, and that final authority on human behavior, the Holy Bible.

Anyway, I used to close at ten o'clock. I wasn't about to shake up the neighbors and risk any squeals to the cops. So to fill up the mammoth gap in my education, I went to bed with a pile of books, and before I was twenty, I was the best-read lady bootlegger west of Belle Livingstone. I learned my arithmetic at the cash register, chemistry I picked up in my bathtub gin experiments, my customers taught me the rudiments of psychology—everything else I knew at that time I learned from books. And they were better than cold baths to fight off the ghost of the nonexistent man in my life.

But you can fool your libido for only just so long. Maybe *you* can outwit *your* yen for someone with whom to share a tube of toothpaste, a pot roast, or Christmas Eve, but *I* got restless. I was twenty: a good-looking twist with a Filipino chauffeur for the white Packard and a growing lump under my mattress that wasn't cotton batting. But I just wasn't satisfied. I wanted something, something different. Then I met Ernest Spagnoli.

Ernest, an attorney from San Francisco, dropped into my place in Ventura the morning after I had had a visit from the Prohis (Prohibition Officers), and although my trusted German shepherd watchdog, Max, seemed to give this tall, good-looking guy the o.k., I had reason to be a little suspicious.

The evening before, the Prohis had arrived in exactly the same type of vehicle, a long black Dodge touring car with side curtains. Of course, they hadn't found anything because I had planted all the hooch in the back yard under some rose bushes. I had learned a *little* from those crummy carrots in Oregon.

So when Ernest first arrived at my place I was a little more than just leery. There wasn't anything in the house by the time he arrived anyway, so after checking his driver's license, fishing license, California Bar license and everything else he possessed, including his money, I told him to wait outside in his car and I'd come out and talk to him. I figured that the distance between my door and his car would give me a running chance to get inside and slam the door if he tried to close that gap.

In the front seat of his car, we had quite a conversation. He was trying to locate a dame named Zelda Woodhayse (believe it or not) who had fleeced one of his Greek clients out of $1,700 in Vallejo. She probably got him before he got her, which pleased me inwardly no end.

I told him that I hadn't seen or heard of the twist, but I was finally convinced that this handsome stranger was all right, and I invited him into the house for a cup of coffee.

He had rented the Dodge from the local taxi station in town and told me that he had to leave that evening to try a case down in Los Angeles. By some strange but true coincidence, I had to be in L.A. too to fight a traffic case in court the next day. I had already given an attorney a $75 retainer fee and I owed him $75 more.

Ernest eyed the white Packard in the driveway and when I told him it was mine, he suggested that we drive to L.A. together. He also said he'd be glad to try my case for free. Even though I had parted with $75 for another attorney, I figured taking this guy up on the deal would save me the rest. I accepted. At least half of his proposition. I couldn't tell *him*, but I had just cooked twenty chickens for my drinking customers who would arrive that evening and I wouldn't be able to leave until after midnight. I found out that if I fed the customers they drank more.

So it was decided that he would take the train to L.A. that evening and I would meet him there the next day. He not only agreed to try my case for nothing despite the loss of a free ride, but said that he'd make arrangements for me to have a room for my chauffeur and myself at the Rosslyn Hotel. You can't beat a deal like *that*.

The next day Ernest tried my case in court, and it didn't cost me a cent. And, like most things you get for nothing, I lost. The judge fined me $500 (he must have heard about the white Packard), or thirty days in jail. Just as I was ready to "thank" Ernest for all he didn't do for me, he did the damnedest thing I ever saw. He reached into his pocket and brought out five crisp new one hundred dollar bills and deposited the bail.

Now this is a really nice guy, I thought to myself, and as he handed the money to the clerk, he told the judge that he would appeal the case. He did, and won it on appeal some time later.

Gone were my inhibitions. Vanished was my vendetta against men; disappeared forever were my unpleasant memories of Le-Roy and Dan; five hundred dollars for a perfectly strange girl. The mind reels! It was right out of King Arthur and the Knights of the Round Table. Talk about shining-armor-clad heroes storming the tower to save a damsel. This guy was Gala-had, plus. I was hooked, but good.

The least I could do was stay around town a few days and let him wine and dine me.

Ernest had made reservations for me at the hotel like he said he would, but when I checked in, the clerk looked up at me, smiled and said, "Glad to have you visit us, Mrs. Spagnoli." That crack put me on my guard and I wasn't but half surprised when I walked into my room (a double by some coincidence) and there stood Ernest. He had made arrangements for my chauffeur down the hall.

After I explained in several well-chosen words that he had wasted his time and money on the wrong girl, he stayed the gentleman he was and moved into other quarters.

For three days Los Angeles was opened up for me, and Ernest took me to the best restaurants and nightclubs, treated me like a lady, and made me like men (or at least one man) all over again. Finally I drove him to Santa Barbara where he was to catch a train for San Francisco to try another case the next morning; and on the way he did the strangest thing I'd ever seen. He proposed. Out of the blue sky, he looked over at me and said, "You're a pretty nice kid, I like you—let's get married."

He hadn't tried any shenanigans, and I had always wanted to see his hometown, San Francisco, so I gave the proposal some thought (about nine seconds' worth) and said yes. We stopped in Ventura, got a marriage license, got a justice of the peace, and got married. Then, I drove my newly begotten husband to Santa Barbara and put him on the train to San Francisco and returned to my little house of high-priced hooch in Ventura.

Wouldn't you know it? Business was better than ever!

Ernest had no idea, of course, what business I was in and I kind of hated to leave my customers and their cash, but he kept sending me telegrams and letters telling me to get my young self to San Francisco. Finally, he sent a wire saying that if I didn't drop everything and join him pronto, he would come and get me. I sure as hell couldn't have him find out my methods of making money so I packed up the lump in my mattress, poured out the hooch and left Ventura to join my husband by the San Francisco Bay.

Besides, I remembered what a great guy he was for putting up the five hundred and figured, "What the hell! Why not?" I knew now that my marriage was going to last forever, and I was equally sure that San Francisco was the answer to all my restless nights and needs. I was half right. I guess that's all you can ask in the way of odds in this life.

Three

THEY were a wonderful set of burglars, the people who were running San Francisco when I first came to town in 1923, wonderful because, if they were stealing, they were doing it with class and style. When they turned City Hall and the Hall of Justice into a pair of stores with bargains for all, they did it with charm, finesse, and what the French call "savoir-faire."

They were the municipal swashbucklers and the civic highbinders. And compared with today's local statesmen, they didn't really try very hard to be much else, except just before election. This is understandable. The politics of the town were dominated by Mayor Jimmy Rolph (Sunny Jim, or Dirty Jim, depending upon where you sat politically), but believe me, he was a doll, a political dreamboat. Say what you will for New York's Jimmy Walker or Boston's Jim Curley, Jimmy Rolph wore San Francisco like a tailor-made plaid suit and on him it looked wonderful. Not only did Jimmy do o.k., but the rest of us did pretty well too. For if there ever was a live-and-let-live type, it was Mayor Rolph of San Francisco. At one time in his colorful career, when asked to make a statement about prostitution he said,

"Leave it alone; just regulate it." That was his motto. Although the old Barbary Coast was gone, the town was spinning just as lustily as it always had—ever since the first pirate stepped down the gangplank from his ship, looked around, and ordered a passing Indian to bring on the women.

The Tenderloin was teeming with prosperity. French restaurants with private rooms and acquiescent ladies upstairs abounded. The North Beach or Italian District for years had been given over to the sober intercourses of industrious Neopolitan fishermen, hardworking broken-English purveyors of salami and Gorgonzolla, and respectable Mafia types who spent their time playing bocce ball and beating their wives. Now it bubbled with alcoholic activity. Speakeasies, wine flats and nightclubs were plentiful. Even in the conservative financial district and practically every premise in town where more than three men might congregate simultaneously, a Klondike game awaited, a game of chance where you throw a dozen dice out of a box to a layout, hoping that the proprietor will pay you a certain amount of money in the event that you shoot unlikely totals. Men loved it; no fortunes were lost, and some were made. Made by the proprietors, that is. All this was done pretty much out in the open with God and Jimmy Rolph looking on.

The love business flourished too.

It should be stated at this point that it was easier to come by professional female company in San Francisco than it was to catch a rash in a leper colony. Not in St. Mary's Cathedral during services and not on election day when every right-minded, hustling gal was out voting for Jimmy Rolph. But there was plenty of stuff around. A curious "coincidence" about it is that the statistics on rape were lowest then on a per capita basis than they ever have been since. Molestation and attacks by reason of perversion were 11 percent per capita of what they were

25 years later at the time when Police Chief Charles Dullea announced the end of prostitution in San Francisco!

But one thing was certain in those days: San Francisco was an open town and the people were happy about it.

Like Rolph said, pleasure wasn't prevented; it was regulated. Such regulation had to be organized and paid for. It was. There were price tags on most things and usually the tab was fair. Now and then, unfortunately, some hungry cop or city hall hog would declare his own little personal markup and then there would be a hassle, but mostly things jogged along on a cash-and-carry basis. There were few complaints.

It's all very well in righteous retrospect to give the rap to corrupt officials, but this is a lot of borscht. This particular period of permissiveness lasted for more than thirty years. Nothing lasts that long unless the people are willing that it should. The people of that San Francisco liked a free-and-easy town. They were not shocked by the facts of life. They were apparently disinterested in a blue-law town. They turned down, year after year at the polls, every clown who sought office on a clean-up ticket.

World War II brought an entirely new species of San Franciscan to town. Fascinated by what they saw in our town on their way to Guadalcanal and Okinawa, thousands of young servicemen returned to Paducah, Peoria, and Pocatello, packed up their wives and goods, and headed back to the Golden Gate town to stay.

They also packed up and brought their Midwest or down East small-town standards too, the jerks. As soon as they had established enough residence to enable them to vote, they voted like the provincials they were for purity and started the destruction of the spirit of the colorful city that had fascinated them. These are the people who claim that some of us debase ourselves by calling the town "Frisco." The real San Franciscans from Charles Cora to Fog Horn Murphy have never called it anything *but* Frisco.

I was determined to be a helluva housewife when I arrived at the other livelier San Francisco as the newly wed Mrs. Ernest Spagnoli. I had a new role to play. I left my business in Ventura and burned another bridge behind me.

Ernest rented an apartment at the Huntington, one of the newest Nob Hill luxury towers. The Mark Hopkins was going up half a block away, and I wasn't at all unaware of my new grandeur.

I was determined to make a hundred-percent-pure-double-dipped housewife in spades. I would cook pot roasts, iron the shirts, and even play mah-jongg with the people next door if necessary. By comparison, I was determined to make Prudence Penny look like Madame Bovary. I had resolved to be so damned respectable that the local minister would think twice before trying to sell me a ticket to the church raffle.

It soon became clear that paying the Huntington rentals was not the best way to help my rising young attorney on his climb to the top. I suggested a home of our own in the Sunset District —the epitome of middle-class respectability. Believe me, no scarlet woman ever set up housekeeping in the Sunset—except me.

All of us respectable ladies followed the same routine. We got out a huge wash Monday morning and hung it in the damp fog-laden Pacific breezes on clotheslines that sagged down between a narrow back porch and the garden back fence twenty yards away. We waxed the floors and polished silver and dusted the bric-a-brac until hell wouldn't have it. Twice a week, when there were changes in the program, we went to the Balboa Theater and watched Conway Tearle or Elsie Ferguson or Harold Lloyd and the travelogues by Burton Holmes. The cleaning woman came in once a week for fifty cents an hour, her lunch and carfare. She helped beat the rugs and shake the furnace ashes and wash the goddamn windows. Once a week we dolled up and, feeling like we'd just arrived from another planet, went downtown to shop on Grant Avenue, have lunch at Townsends, and buy a slip at the City of Paris.

From that home in the Sunset we graduated to another place in the Sherwood Forest District. Everything went along fairly well, but I began to have that feeling of incompleteness again. I thought I had the answer and told Ernest that I wanted to adopt a son.

I made arrangements with a woman who had one too many to handle during those depression years of 1929. I took the little fellow home to love and cuddle and that's when all hell broke loose.

Around that time my darling husband had become the heir to a sizable fortune left him from the Doctor Sands estate in Pittsburgh, Pennsylvania. His dear, charming sister, who had never had any great love for me (except when I went to her house to clean her kitchen or make her beds) pointed out to Ernest how "permanent" adopting a child was. She was good enough to explain what I had never felt was important enough to consider— that an adopted child had all the legal rights of one that had been born to us. What she was so concerned about was the possibility of my newfound son and I dipping into the new inheritance till. It wasn't as big a problem as she thought because I had the answer ready for her.

"We can solve this whole thing very easily," I said. "Ernest can keep the money and I'll take the child."

Ernest and I tried to mend the fences because I knew he loved me and I had come to love him, but sometimes it's better to leave one another while there's still some respect left. Perhaps that's why we still love and respect each other today.

With the few dollars I had left over from my Ventura enterprise, I bought a little hotel at 693 O'Farrell Street and wondered why in hell I had ever left the hooch business in the first place. It was 1929.

I'd been sprung from the household drudgery and routine and spared the further criticisms of Ernest's family. I had learned early in life to keep my lips sealed. Even a fish wouldn't get caught if he kept his mouth shut. San Quentin is full of people who have talked their way in and have nothing left to talk their way out with.

Ernest's family was always a little suspicious of me: whether or not I came from the proper lineage and what my background really was. I never enlightened them any. I kept my car in the name of Marcia Wells, in case the hotel went under. If *that* didn't go, I'd at least have something to drive off a cliff with.

When that fateful day came and two policemen, McCausland and his partner, Bartell, entered the hotel and asked for Marcia Wells, I knew it must have something to do with the beautiful new yellow Lincoln Le Baron sedan parked at the curb.

"She isn't in," I said, not sure if they believed me or not. After two or three return visits and a little checking on the part of the Police Department, Officer McCausland returned and appeared more than just unhappy with me.

"All right," he said, "I know you are Marcia Wells. You're under arrest."

"For what?" I shot back.

"For leaving your car parked on the street all night" said McCausland.

Remembering the fingerprints from Oregon and not wanting my prison stint ever to be made public, I didn't have any desire to be taken downtown and booked. I grabbed the telephone and began to dial a bail bondsman, Billy Lyons.

Just that morning I had had a cast removed from my right arm, which had been broken some time earlier when I tripped on a rug and took a tumble at the foot of the stairs. McCausland moved like a leopard and, in his polite and gentlemanly way, twisted and rebroke my damn arm. He took me from the house and down to the station on Bush Street. By the time I got there my arm was swollen like a weather balloon clear down to my wrist.

The desk sergeant, being at least half human, sent me home from the station without the necessity of being booked downtown. This infuriated Cop McCausland who felt I had given him a rougher time than his authority deserved.

Once home I called Ernest and, as usual, he came quickly to my defense. He threatened to take McCausland and his partner Bartell before the Police Commission for cruelty charges.

By this time Ernest had achieved some reputation for his defense of "Spud" Murphy, "Kayo" Kavoski and a guy named Gary, who were supposed to have raped some dame down south of Market Street. News was scarce at the time and all the press played hell out of the story. All the Women's Leagues and churchgoers attended the trials to hear any little tidbits they could.

Ernest was always a fighter. He'd fight just as hard for some poor slob who hadn't a nickel as he would for those with the dough. Many reforms were made in California because of his efforts. The first all-woman jury in the state was set up by him in the Casper-Franta murder trial. The first writ of Certiorari (review) from the Supreme Court of California to the United States Supreme Court in Washington in forty years was won by him in the Isaac Wolfgang case. Wolfgang was nabbed by a policeman while trying to steal a bottle of milk. He hadn't a dime to his name and tried to stay alive in the only way he knew. The police officer took him to his shabby little room and in searching it (for what, I'll never know—maybe bread to go with the milk) he found a revolver in a drawer. A scuffle occurred and the officer was shot and killed. Ernest didn't try the case but he picked up the cudgel after Wolfgang had been convicted. No one was more surprised than he when, just a few days before the scheduled execution, the California Supreme Court granted his writ of review. Ernest flew to Washington on his own time and money to defend his writ in front of the United States Supreme Court. He lost, goddamn it, but he tried like hell.

So, it was found out who I was, and the law seemed to try even harder to get *something* on me. They hated to think that I would get away with anything without having to pay the protection that everyone else was spreading around.

I had bought the hotel from Ella Yates. Before I purchased the place she showed me around and it was full of linen—towels, blankets, and pillow slips—all necessary in the hotel business. After I had bought the place the inventory suddenly diminished to two dishcloths and a napkin. I couldn't have kept a baby polar bear warm. I refused to pay her the mortgage until she returned all the linen she had scaffled.

When I took possession, I inherited a headache by the name of Jean Porter, a Russian twist who gave me a bad taste in my mouth about Russians that I've never forgotten. She not only never paid the rent, but she brought up every soldier, sailor, and anything else with two legs and loose, to her room—which was bad for my business.

I remember one day asking my housekeeper, Kitty Hawkins, if she knew what went with Jean Porter.

"Have you looked in her room lately?" I asked.

The Lady of the House

"No," Kitty said, "I haven't even seen her."

My warning mechanism that operates somewhere in my head kept telling me something was wrong. We went to her room, opened it with a passkey and I found that my hunch was right.

On the bed, soaked with her own blood, was Jean. She had tried to abort herself and messed up badly. I called an ambulance, contacted a doctor named Bernstein at Sutter Hospital whom I knew and who in turn saved her life. I topped that off by paying all the doctor and hospital bills.

She finally got out of the hospital and went back to work as a presser at Alex's Pressing and Cleaning Establishment. (She was a fancy presser, among other things.) The only reason I had for wanting to help that girl was my knowledge of her six-month-old baby whom she boarded out. In payment (which I didn't expect anyhow) for whatever I might have done for her, she slipped out in the middle of the night. She went to Ella Yates' hotel, of all places. Ella was a dear friend of McCausland's. It was inevitable that this improbable trio got their knobby heads together and figured out how to frame me. Believe me, they tried like hell.

They tried everything known to science to nail me with a legitimate pinch. Policemen began to enter the hotel early and late, every time they saw a potential roomer come in off the streets. They never found anything. I had a cash register and a license and hardly enough profits to pay my own rent.

But one day they got the break they were waiting for. A young and beautiful blond girl and a charming guy came to the hotel and asked me if I had a room to rent. I said that I did, and for four dollars a week I rented one to them. The young man was a doctor's son from Redlands and his pretty, blond wife was a Swedish girl from San Francisco with a very well-connected father. Her marriage just hadn't pleased the old folks and the kids were trying to stay out of their way and trouble. Seeing this lovely girl and her husband, the cops put 2 plus 2 together and came up , as usual, with 69.

One evening when I wasn't there they sent two little juvenile delinquents to my hotel to get a girl, rent a room, or anything else they could get away with. Coppers McCausland and Bartell waited patiently outside.

This time the fit really hit the shan. The two little punks identified that nice Swedish kid as the girl that "propositioned" them. There was a big vice raid and the news hit the headlines like Hiroshima: WIFE OF PROMINENT ATTORNEY ARRESTED FOR RUNNING DISORDERLY HOUSE.

Every S.O.B. in the Police Department got in the act. There was Captain Dullea, Captain Goff, and sweet little Jean Porter.

That daffy Russki claimed that she had lived at my hotel and had been working for me as a prostitute. She said, in detail, that I had sent her to a room, had put a towel in her hand and that she picked up two dollars from the guy inside. Two dollars!! Keerist! Had she said fifty I wouldn't have felt so bad. Two dollars is a little unthinkable, even during the depression.

I was charged with everything from "keeping a house" to "pandering" and the gendarmes even hired Jake Ehrlich as Special Prosecutor.

Somehow they got wind of the baby, but before they could take him away too, I got him to my mother in Oregon to keep until the mess was over. I was one step ahead of them that time, but not enough ahead. While I was in Oregon they came to my house in Sherwood Forest (when Ernest and I separated I kept the house and he kept his sister), and they gathered up my sixteen-year-old kid brother who was staying with me while he went to school.

When I arrived back home, I looked through the house and no brother. I frantically called my mother in hopes he had decided to go home to Oregon. No such luck. I jumped in my car and drove to Galileo High School and looked everywhere for him. Finding a kid at a high school is worse than looking for the proverbial needle, but I finally located him.

He hardly knew me, or at least, that's how he acted. He couldn't talk to me. I demanded that he get into the car and I took him to my older brother's apartment and asked him what he was doing, where he was staying and why. He confessed to me that the Police Department, while I was gone, had come to the house and made arrangements for him to stay at a house on Maple Street.

It was a little hard for me to understand. In fact, it was impossible. I had caddied on the golf course to buy his baby food and clothes when he was born. I'd loved him and cared for him all his life, and now he was acting like I was poison, working with the crooked scheme to frame me. But there was more to it than just that.

He wanted to be a commercial artist and so I'd sent him to a California School of Fine Arts. While he was there, he met a captain in the Marine Corps by the name of Ralph R. Dustan, a member of a socially prominent family in Beverly Hills. I couldn't believe what I was hearing. He told me the whole sordid story. I felt as though my heart was being ripped out of my chest.

I begged him to leave, to go home to his mother and leave all this behind. He promised me that he would, but first he had to go to Maple Street and gather up all his belongings. We planned to meet, and I told him I would make all the arrangements for him. It would be all right. It *had* to be.

It wasn't. He never showed up for the meeting.

Instead, I was promptly arrested for the attempted bribery of my brother. As soon as I got out on bail, I was out looking for him again. I followed McCausland, Jake Ehrlich, Captain Goff, and the rest every waking hour until I found where they had stashed him.

I called my mother at once. He being a minor, I wanted to avoid any more trouble, so I took Mother along for the meeting. He didn't expect us.

He was staying at the home of a man named Sandsetter on Vienna Street, and my mother and I waited for hours in the chilled rainy darkness in front of Sandsetter's home until, finally, my brother arrived. We had been crouched in the bushes and as he came closer to the front door of the house I stepped out of the bushes in front of him. He dashed for the front door and tried to close it in my face, but I forced it open. He stepped back inside and I held the door open while Mother entered the front hallway. For a long second his eyes met hers and mountains of words tried to pass between them. But there were no words that could express how I felt, how my mother felt, and I suppose how he must have felt too.

Sandsetter asked us all into the kitchen and there, over coffee, we tried to talk the whole thing out. I knew that Sandsetter would not call the police, but it did not matter to me if he did or didn't. I'd talked to him earlier in the evening before my brother had finally come home and he told me that he had been staying out late nights. Sandsetter didn't approve, but he could do nothing to prevent it. He couldn't understand why my brother would want to testify against his own sister. Neither did I.

My mother looked across the table at my brother's face. Somehow, he didn't look the same to me. He looked almost like a stranger. The involvement with the Marine, Captain Dustan, had done something to him.

"Son, why are you doing this terrible thing?" Mother asked.

He looked up, shaking his head slowly from side to side, trying to avoid my eyes. "I lon't know, I don't know," he said.

We talked for endless minutes, perhaps hours, trying to show him that he was making the most terrible mistake of his life.

Mother reached across the table and touched his hand lightly. "Son," she said quietly, as a mother does when she knows that something is wrong deep in the mind of her child, "son, your sister loves you. Marcy *loves* you. All your life she's tried to *do* for you, just as though you were her very own son and not her brother. Please . . . please come home with me and forget all this. Come home with your mother."

The tears welled up in my brother's eyes and he began to shake all over. He began to cry. I wanted to reach out to him. He grabbed at my mother's hand, squeezing it tighter and tighter and nodded his head, hard. "Yes, all right," he said finally, "I'll go home, Ma-ma." I put a hand over my face and tried to hold back the sob that mounted in my throat and stifled my words. This time he will keep his word; he *will* go home, I thought. He said that he first must take care of some business in the morning and then he would go home. He kept his word, but he didn't go home; and at that moment I had no *idea* what that "business" was.

He met Ralph R. Dustan, who was feverishly trying to get a transfer to China. Had I known as much then as I do now, I would have taken care of Marine Captain Dustan!

With the full knowledge and approval of the Police Department, Dustan had made an allotment to my brother of $60 a month. I didn't know it then, but I soon found out. My brother wanted to go somewhere else. Not home. I suggested Reno. I don't know why.

I flew ahead of him and made a place for him to stay, cautioning him about telephone calls and about not being seen on the streets at this crucial time. The police had convinced my brother to lie on the stand about my business to build a better case for themselves. They obviously had caught Dustan and my brother in a compromising situation and used that as the sword over his head.

So, for a while, my brother stayed in Reno and was safe. But he suddenly became bored. He wanted to go to Los Angeles. Reno was "too cold, too dull." He asked me for some money to finance his trip and sent me the allotment check Dustan had sent to him and asked me to sign it and cash it for him. I did.

I sent him the money as soon as I could cash the check and he went to Los Angeles. He began to make long-distance calls to Dustan and the calls finally tipped off the authorities to where he was staying. They brought him back to San Francisco.

This time around, my brother was to be the star witness. It wasn't just for trying to bribe him that the law was going to get me. It was for the "forgery" of the check I had cashed for him. And *he* was going to testify that it was true!

When I heard this news, I remembered back to when I met my brother for the first time during this trouble at Galileo High School. I had written him a thirteen-page letter that very night, and I vividly remember one part in particular. It read:

> My dear Brother:
>   Looking over the papers and paintings and things from the past that remind me so much of you, I can't help but feel that down deep in your heart, under your mask of utter indifference, there must be something left in your heart for me.

The next time I saw that letter was during my trial in Federal Court for forgery of a government check—a federal charge that would mean the penitentiary if I lost. I looked across the courtroom, on the other side of the hall, and saw my brother. The same flesh, the same blood, the same memories; and now two complete worlds apart from one another.

He had turned the letter over to the Police Department as evidence of my handwriting as compared to that on the government allotment check. An anger began to build inside me. Not against my brother, but against the police who used him and the Government that would allow themselves to be used in such a shabby manner. The anger built inside me, overcoming all other emotions, and I knew I *had* to win.

Albert Bagshaw, who later became the District Attorney of Marin County and subsequently a partner in a law firm there, was a young Deputy United States District Attorney in the Federal Courts of San Francisco, and he was picked to try the case. He fought with the vehemence that came from knowing the feather that would be placed in his barrister's bonnet if he could convict me.

The only sample of my signature being the letter to my brother, Bagshaw introduced it into evidence. He made one mistake then that I know he never made again during his career. He did not restrict the entering of the letter into evidence only so far as my handwriting was concerned. He submitted the letter itself, including its contents.

My attorney, Nat Coughlin, jumped to his feet, ran over to my side and whispered in my ear, "Should I object to the letter being introduced into evidence?"

"My God no," I said. "Just hope that Bagshaw doesn't get smart before the Court rules it into evidence in total."

The letter went into great length about the details of the case, including everyone and his ancestors that were connected with it. It talked about Dustan, the Special Prosecutor Jake Ehrlich, the check from the Government, and, in short, the actual truth about everything.

The letter was read to the Court.

Coughlin, in the golden oratory for which he was so famous, told the stern-faced jury in his closing argument that "there are two roads open" for me. He went on to say, "You must decide whether this young girl shall go to prison, or home to her young son."

Bagshaw objected immediately, and rightfully. You cannot comment or instruct the jury on prison and matters of penalty. The judge held with Bagshaw, but made one remark:

"The Court," he said, "may have something to say about this case later."

The judge who tried my case was Harold McCormick. Judge Kerrigan, whom I was to have originally, had taken a sudden leave of absence. He did not want to judge this particular case. He knew my husband Ernest very well. He often stayed at the home of my husband and my brother-in-law's sister at Lake Tahoe. Throughout the trial, Ernest sat on the sidelines and I never felt so terribly sorry for anyone in my life. To watch his career go down the drain because of a miserable bunch of liars and a greedy handful of cops. His career, however, was saved, for I was acquitted by the jury of all charges within thirty minutes.

During the trial proceedings, I found and acquired about twenty letters from Dustan to my brother. They were full of information about the case against me, named the names and gave the facts. I still have those letters.

After the trial there was another Grand Jury hearing that lasted all night. Frank Eckenroth was the head of that jury. He was one of the kindest men I've ever known. I sat in muted silence, the old swelling coming to my eyes and throat again as I heard the letters read aloud to the jury, which listened with rapt attention until they were all finished. There was a silence in the room that was deafening.

When it was over, August Fortner, who was the Deputy District Attorney in charge of Grand Jury affairs for that evening, quickly called for a recess. Frank Eckenroth, bless his heart, put his arms around my shaking shoulders and called a cab to take me home. He told me to get some sleep. He knew I damn well needed it.

The Lady of the House

After I had gone home, the Grand Jury went back into their deliberations and before morning wanted to indict everyone and anyone who had anything to do with the case against me. The letters to my brother, explaining how easy it would be to frame me and how the police would take care of everything, naming the people involved and how they did it all, was all any Grand Jury needed to shake up the Police Department, the District Attorney's office and all the rest of the S.O.B.'s involved. Perjury and the dissemination of it was, and are, serious offenses indeed.

But August Fortner's persuasiveness prevailed and they failed to reach any indictments against anyone, including me, for whom the stage had been originally set.

Years later, I saw an ad in the paper mentioning that the Grand Jury Badge of Gold that belonged to Frank Eckenroth was on sale at a pawnshop on Kearny Street. I went down immediately to buy it, but someone had gotten there ahead of me. Perhaps it was a member of the family or someone who cared for Frank as I did. It would have been a wonderful memento of a human and wonderful guy. I have often wondered where it is.

So, the trials and the heartache of that period were over for a little while, at least. Janette Proctor was indicted for perjury; McCausland is dead and his partner Bartell has dropped out of sight; Dustan disappeared or went on to mess up the life of some other child, and Ella Yates passed on to some reward. Poor Ella never did get the rest of the mortgage I owed her; and the years went on.

One good thing the experience did for me was to introduce me to a truly fine man and attorney, Jake Ehrlich. Jake did not know what he was getting involved with in this mess, and many years later, when asked during a discussion what was the sorriest thing he ever did, he reached over and took my hand and said,

The Lady of the House

"The sorriest thing I ever did was to prosecute Sally Stanford."
And I know he meant every word of it.

One bad thing did happen. That American Beauty Quick Heating Electric Iron finally caught up with me again. During the court trial Sheriff John R. Terrell was imported from Oregon to identify me as the person who had served that little stint at Salem. Now it was out in the open. Ex-con! And it lived with me for most of my life, always a dark shadow on the brightest day. A deep and piercing scar that was to take twenty-seven and a half years to heal.

Years later, I contacted my young brother and told him of our mother's passing. He, and all the lambs of the family, black and white, stood around the casket in a little white mortuary in Medford, Oregon.

I looked for long moments at her face, at her white hands and snow-white hair, and slowly turned my head to look upon my brother's face through the glaze that covered my eyes. He stood stock still, his head down, his eyes closed.

Cool rain was falling as I walked from the chapel to my car. I couldn't help but wonder if my brother remembered another rainy day, when his mother stood exposed to the cold night air; if he remembered that she stayed in that rain all night long, just to beg her son to come back home with her. I wonder if he remembered his promise to her and how that word was broken.

Four

THE bridges to the past were burned to a turn, and those readers who are unable to understand why I felt that my past was as old as last week's tamales just don't understand two very concrete realities of life. At least of *my* life.

One is that being labeled a "Madam" is quite different from being accused of being a thief or a murderer. A prominent San Francisco jeweler I know once served time in San Quentin for theft. It is forgotten. Our community's greatest attorney served two penitentiary terms. Hardly a soul remembers that. A restaurateur with a thousand friends in the town's financial district was convicted of robbery when he was very young. I'll give you odds that none of his thousands of friends know of it. Two ex-San Francisco mayors had brushes with the law, one for a sex offense. Who knows and who cares? Apparently no one. But let a woman be accused . . . not convicted, just accused . . . of a crime involving sex and no one *ever* forgets it. And no one ever misses an opportunity to pass it along to his friends, acquaintances and for that matter, total strangers. It's too good a conversation piece, too great as gossip material and too spicy a label with which to categorize a woman.

The Lady of the House

Any woman accused learns this immutable law of life at the time, and either allows it to destroy her or makes the most of it —as I did.

The other concrete reality that requires understanding is that Ernest's family, like most every other family, must have felt that I was beyond redemption. Where there was all this smoke, there must have been some fire.

It was an impossible situation.

Right or wrong, and on the basis of the unfriendly facts that faced me after the arrest, I figured I had no chance of lasting as the wife of a coming young attorney. I had been put in the business of being a madam without being consulted. I could spend the rest of my life vainly denying a lie that many people would prefer to believe. Or, I could turn the lie into a truth that would earn me the means of protection from such people. I chose the latter course. I vowed to be the best damn madam in town. And I made it.

At this point, I am aware that certain readers will shake their pointy little heads, smite their foreheads and demand to know if that awful Stanford woman doesn't realize that she's a sinner. Well, there's a Book that says we're all sinners and I at least chose a sin that's made quite a few people happier than they were before they met me, a sin that's left me with very little time to consider other extremely popular moral misdemeanors, like usury, intolerance, bearing false tales, extortion, racial bigotry, and the casting of that first stone. And, I might add, a hell of a lot worse.

Unlike Lot's wife, I never looked back once I became a full-fledged citizen of San Francisco's Tenderloin. The first thing I needed was a new name. I couldn't use Marcia Spagnoli without embarrassing poor Ernest. I was damn good and sure I wasn't going to be Marcia Busby again and give my already oversensitive relatives something further to come out at the seams about.

The Lady of the House

It so happened that I was faced with this momentous decision on the weekend of the University of California-Stanford football game. I was still in the Sherwood Forest home. Washing my hair and taking a bath usually lifts me out of the blues, but on this foggy, lonely Saturday afternoon, it helped not a bit. I felt lousy. I was depressed. I was at loose ends. I'd put on my favorite dress, my handsomest hat, and walked over to Harry Marquard's for dinner, picking up a late edition of the *Bulletin* on the way.

Marky's was always gay, and I felt better at once. I searched through the theater ads in the paper for a pleasant way to spend the evening. The band that entertained before show time was playing a familiar tune, but its name eluded me. I found out that Ethel Barrymore was playing at the Columbia Theater next door in *Declassé*. Well, what do you know? As I tried to make up my mind whether or not I should have myself a look at Miss Barrymore's idea of a "declassé" woman, the name of the song being played came to me. It was "I Wonder What's Become of Sally?"—a good question, and a good name for a gal who might have people wondering what became of her. Then I noticed the headline on my newspaper—STANFORD BEATS CALIFORNIA. Well, if Stanford could beat California (my adversary, "The People of," versus little old me), I was all for Stanford, and suddenly I had a new name.

I went to the telephone and asked the box office at the Columbia if there was a single seat for *Declassé*. The treasurer said that there was and for whom should he reserve it. "For Sally Stanford," I replied. Little did the man know that he had participated not only in a ticket sale, but a christening ceremony as well.

When I received the little white envelope enclosing the ducat, I eyed it with considerable curiosity. It is odd to see your name, written out, for the first time in your life.

The Lady of the House

Next, the job of starting a really productive business. San Francisco was the last major city in the United States in which commercial society and vice were frank and open commodities. No man had to respond to a furtive whisper in an alley in order to get a drink, a girl, or a chance at a full house. After all, this was the end of 1931.

The Tenderloin cafés were famous and not only for flamboyant activities. Spider Kelly's at Mason and Ellis had entertainment that would nowadays be playing Las Vegas. The Bay City Grill served a porterhouse and a planked steak that drew praise from gourmets all over the world. The plank steak was served on a block of charred oak. It was fenced in with an inch-high edge of sculptured mashed potatoes. New York or Paris offered nothing better.

Bones Remmer's Menlo Club on Eddy Street around the corner from the old Tivoli Opera House, or the play at Kingston or the Chad Milligan's, drew the best gamblers in the country—Titanic Thompson, Nick the Greek, Eddy Sahati, even the famed Rothsteins from New York. The local sportsmen, Freddy the Glut, Jelly and Marty Breslauer, Ziggy Rosener, Ten Grand Patty (whose brother is a prominent lawyer in San Francisco), Carnation Willie, Russian Mike, Benny the Gent, and Joe Bernstein, the Silver Fox, regarded themselves just as classy as anything the national or international gambling circuit could offer. None of them asked or gave quarter nor reduced the odds or the stakes. They were all wonderful people and most of them became my clients and friends.

Excitement? You can be sure of that. Here was fine food, entertainment as good as any on Broadway, and the only concession to legal propriety was a house rule that all liquor should be served from the floor, from beneath the customers' tables. At Coffee Dan's down on O'Farrell you were given a wooden hammer along with your silverware, and you could bang your fool head off to the tunes and sometimes improvised lyrics of Frankie Shaw and Les Poe. Fanchon and Marco had recently graduated from dancing at Tait's where there was a busboy by the name of Rudolph Valentino; but Fanchon's brother, Rube Woolf, had the band in the upstairs cabaret called The Plantation. A stripper, Sally Rand, would twirl a large fan over her shapely fanny in this same room in the years to come.

There was no closing hour at Dutch White's at 110 Eddy Street, where most of the hustlers spent their hard-earned money long after their tricks had gone home to their carping wives and the early-morning alarm clocks and the dirty dishes in the sink. Shanty Malone, a crazy Irishman whose only idols were athletes, owned half the speakeasies in town and kept opening and closing his string of saloons because it was more convenient to open and close than to pay off all the different kinds of officials and near officials and friends of officials including the cops who added their names to the tribute list.

Particularly characteristic of San Francisco's Tenderloin were the French restaurants: St. Germaine, Pierre's, The Poodle Dog, Blanco's and many others. The particular characteristic of the French restaurants was neither the sauces nor the accents of the maître-d', but rather the rooms and the bedrooms upstairs. Many a patrician San Francisco woman scabbed in The Profession in one of these discreet private dining rooms. But who could be critical of the amateurs when one considers the many phone calls one got to provide dinner dates at twenty-five dollars an hour for guests in these same rooms?

The Poodle Dog boasted an elevator in which the ladies could be speeded to the scene of action. And Blanco's went further; it had an elevator so large that a car or a cab with its occupants could be driven into it and be delivered almost to the door behind which the impatient male waited. A girl who handled such an engagement could say afterwards quite literally that she had been driven into a life of sin. The very proper Moose Lodge now occupies that building.

There were these and a thousand more gay, lively places. But the lifeblood of the Tenderloin was the girls, and almost every hotel or apartment in the mile square of the region housed a hospitality center where a lonesome male might prove his manhood and find solace and comfort.

In years before and immediately after the earthquake, the ladies had vended their wares elsewhere in the town. Previously most of the bordellos had been located in the area around the Barbary Coast, Kearny Street, and in Maiden Lane, which is now a smart shopping thoroughfáre.

Strangely enough, a Protestant minister is given credit for having been responsible for the move to what became the Tenderloin. This gentleman was the Reverend Paul Smith and his church was at Geary and Mason streets. Brother Smith, it appeared, had been solicited one night by some nearsighted prostitute. The offer shook him up immeasurably. The power of an angry, righteous God overwhelmed him, and he climbed into the pulpit the following Sunday and preached a sermon about the awfulness of it all. A newspaper city desk, faced with a news shortage for its Monday morning paper, interviewed Smith and published his traumatic experience in full. They included the precise location where the poor dame wafted temptation beneath his quivering nostrils.

Now the cops had to act. They suspended all action on that block and for good measure two or three adjacent ones. The next Sunday, when Pastor Smith looked out across the lectern, he found for once he had a full house. He was playing to an SRO congregation. But most of the faces that looked up at him were more furious than rapt.

Every woman who had been thrown out of work because of

his most recent labor in the vineyard was present, sitting bolt upright in her pew and looking forward to having a few well-chosen words with the Reverend Paul. Their spokesman was a very articulate woman named Reggie Gamble, and Reggie didn't wait for an invitation! She started the catechism immediately after the last swelling notes of the opening hymn had died away. Miss Gamble stood up and asked what the good people of the church and their shepherd were going to do about some two hundred women from whose mouths the daily bread had been snatched.

Reverend Brother Paul didn't know for sure at that moment, but he felt certain that the good ladies of his congregation would provide something—something respectable.

The good ladies of the congregation were strangely silent as they shot sidelong glances at their pew mates. The minister went on to say something about having faith and everything would come out o.k. because of the well-known love that a neighbor has for a neighbor in this best of worlds.

Well, the unemployed ladies took him at his word. They literally became his neighbors. They moved into every dwelling adjoining the church and damn few of them did any housework. Came "The Fire" and the Good Lord spared neither the church nor the adjoining dwellings. In rebuilding, the Reverend Smith decided on another location. The immigrants liked Mason and Post streets, however, and stayed on. By that time prohibition had come to its high tide and before the reformers had turned the raucous playground into a disinfected wasteland, the San Francisco Tenderloin was all that I've claimed for it, and more.

And it was to these fallow acres that I brought my humble talents after I had found for sure that I was a Madam instead of a Mrs. I took a place in an apartment building at 610 Leavenworth Street. I talked things over with some of the best gals in the profession. I was in business. I want to say here and now that at no time at all did I ever knowingly hire a nonprofessional to work for me. I only wanted girls who knew what they were doing, and I discouraged all amateurs from getting into the business. If they were determined to come into the business, let them serve apprenticeship somewhere else.

I was also determined that if it was a house for erring husbands and disillusioned lovers I was to run, it would have to be the best damn one in the world. I decorated it with stuff from the finest furniture stores in town. I installed a colored maid in uniform. And I instructed her to shut the door in the face of any customer who wasn't gentleman enough to make known his wants in words of more than four letters.

I put in soft music, quiet plumbing, soft lights and Beauty Rest mattresses. I made sure that the back door worked in case the police dropped by. Next to the front door I hung a demure little sign: ROOMS. Then I sat down with my girls. There were six of them, and we waited for the arrival of our first cash customer. We didn't have to wait long.

The bell rang, and the maid ushered in a tall gawky man in a long, green overcoat. I can see him still. I smiled him into a chair and ordered a drink served. He seemed a little bashful and I tried to put him at ease:

"What is your preference?" I asked charmingly.

"Well . . . I'd like a small . . ."

"I'll let you see them all. Company's in the parlor, ladies."

They came in, fingering their back hair and simpering prettily. Our customer appeared flabbergasted by such beauty, and I was a little proud myself.

"Now, which would you prefer?"

The man appeared to be having some trouble finding his voice, but finally he spoke:

"All I want is a small room with a large closet."

And it turned out that that was exactly what the S.O.B. *did* want.

But 610 Leavenworth became a home away from home to many a lonesome character as time went by, and we prospered. There were a lot of things I had to learn and I learned them the hard way. I found out that while fully fifty percent of the girls who became prostitutes were a hundred percent foolish, among the other half were some of the cleverest, most resourceful females I'd ever encountered. I found that I was forever going to have trouble with the men that hustling women support: their pimps.

The word "pimp" is almost never spoken by a prostitute. She calls this creature to whom she gives her leisure time and most of her money "My Old Man," be he nineteen or ninety. The women need these leeches like a turtle needs music lessons; but most of them, sooner or later, show up with a glib male in dame-bought finery who begins to mastermind the career of his protégée. He will ultimately leave her at precisely the point where she is at the lowest ebb of her life, and she will be lucky if he leaves her with enough money for cyanide and carfare to the morgue.

Why these women feel they need such leeches is beyond me. There are as many theories as there are those who think about it. Psychiatrists claim that having "an old man" is merely a form of self-punishment common to most women in one degree or another. I might accept this point of view if I could work up some substantial respect for the psychiatrists themselves, many of whom make headlines for having affairs with their barbers, shoplifting at Macy's, or charging their frustrated female patients for their sexual services on the couch.

Whatever is the cause for the prevalence of pimpery, it is stubbornly there and, come to think of it, it is not restricted to prostitutes. Since I opened the Valhalla Restaurant, I've noticed numbers of wealthy women whose costume accessories include fancy males. Maybe all women who lack the real thing feel the need of a substitute. Perhaps they need someone to despise first thing in the morning.

I learned a lot about men from my customers at 610. I learned to get the money first. Many, especially those with a few drinks, tended to become roguish and waggishly amused at the idea of not paying as soon as they had buttoned up the last button, or zipped the last zipper. Also, there was a chance of drunks passing out and taking up expensive space for the rest of the night.

I learned to avoid the sadists in whom many madams specialize. They are often wealthy and willing to pay premium prices. I have a very vivid memory of one United States senator, during the later and more deluxe days of the Nob Hill House, whose delight was whips. I wasn't at all surprised some years afterward when he made a well-publicized speech advocating the whipping post for bank robbers. It figured. He just couldn't stop mixing business with his pleasure.

I learned that men came to a place such as mine not only for sex but for a whole batch of other reasons: to talk about their troubles, their wives' infidelities; to sleep off a drunk; to find out if there were any new wrinkles; to get laughs for jokes that were clinkers elsewhere; to find sweethearts and even wives; to escape from the cops; to get advice on the cure of social diseases; and some to get a good cup of coffee and a plate of ham and eggs when everything else was closed.

I learned that some of the customers were sheep in wolves' clothing. Like one clown who showed up regularly once a month for more than a year wearing the same sports coat, slacks, the same figured shirt, the ready-made bow tie, and a guilty small boy's expression. The girl he visited told me he was just the

The Lady of the House

same in other dull details. He came to talk about what others came to do. We gave him the nickname of "Tea-for-two" because he would always order up a couple of cups to the room with a tray of sandwiches. That's *all* he wanted, too.

I got curious to find out what was with this citizen. The next time he left, I tailed him (having become a pro at that by this time). He climbed into his late-model Ford. It was a dark and foggy night. He led me out into a remote suburb. When he climbed out of the Ford, plaid jacket and all were gone. Now he was wearing a reversed collar as he demurely let himself into the residence house of a local church.

The next time he showed up I told him, as he paid his dues, that I hoped he hadn't been dipping into the collection plate. He gave me a ghostly grin, spared the girl the usual small talk, and disappeared forever from our midst. I knew what I was doing. Customers like that are no good to a business house that likes to think it has a future; there's always a chance that these monkeys will get religion one day and blow the whistle on you.

And so the time passed, and I learned my lessons from life and became a little wiser and a lot warier—but not wary enough because I fell in love again.

This trip to the halter was with a good-looking young fellow named Lou Rapp. It lasted thirteen years. They were good years and like most husbands, Lou brought with him a lot of fun and a little heartache. In many ways these were the good years of my life. So many things were happening to me and for me.

Five

AND then the Mayor became a customer, though not a guest
at the House, of course. Although he was no stranger to
the Tenderloin, and would stick his neck out if it brought him
closer to a new and beautiful girl, Sunny Jim Rolph was not the
kind to bring his personal business to a house of prostitution.

However, he did a lot of entertaining. Men were his guests
and for such purposes he had leased for his associates a Cau-
casian geisha house at 699 Sanchez Street in the Mission District,
a place that was conveniently remote from his home and wife.
Early one evening, I received a call from Ed Rainey, Rolph's
secretary, aide-de-camp, and chief conniver. It seemed that
three bright, good-natured and able-bodied young ladies were
needed for the comfort and delectation of a covey of politicians
arriving from Los Angeles. I had long been determined to meet
Sunny Jim Rolph. What you know can be helpful, but who you
know even more so. I hoped to meet him under the most favora-
ble circumstances. I chose three elegantly beautiful girls, picked
out a stunning hat and dress for myself and we taxied out to the
Mayor's pleasure palace.

We were met by Rainey, who formerly wrote for the San

Francisco *Examiner* and was a wonderful guy. We were introduced to the guests and an eager bunch of politicians they were.

Boys on the town, such as these, often are devoted to bum jokes and impromptu games of grab-ass that pass for partying. I was about ready to leave the girls to this game when Sunny Jim put in his appearance. I knew immediately why he had beaten his opponent, P. H. "Pinhead" McCarthy, by a 300 percent plurality.

Rolph, who was later to become one of the greatest governors California ever had, was a handsome, charming man whose manner and appearance come back to me each time I see Tennessee Ernie Ford, the entertainer. Jim Rolph was a combination of Jimmy Walker and Jake Ehrlich and Pat Brown and all the other easy charmers. It was almost without effort that he would turn you into a constituent.

Not a large man, he made up for it with a voice that turned the most casual statement into a graceful speech. In some respects he was a sartorial freak, but on him it looked good. He wore a cutaway coat, a black pearl in an impeccably knotted cravat, and he was always seen with a carnation in his lapel. He probably wore one to bed on his pajamas.

He never wore shoes, preferring Western boots with semi-high heels and one trouser cuff draped, Texas style, into the top of the boot. He was probably the last politician in San Francisco to let himself be seen, more than occasionally, in a high silk hat. When he became Governor, he took to wearing huge cattleman's Stetsons. If he'd ever visited India, he'd have worn a turban. He was a hat-minded man.

Sunny Jim's attitudes were the most significant thing about him. First and foremost, he was for Live and Let Live, Let Sleeping Dogs Lie, and Don't Stir Up Muddy Water. Also, If You Haven't Tried It, Don't Knock It. He was for an open town. And the reasonable premise of an open mind plus an open pocketbook was fundamental with him. He was one of the few who could provoke a spontaneous public ovation without sending runners ahead of him to make sure it was spontaneous.

A revealing story about Rolph was told to me by Gene Fowler, the writer, while stimulating his arteries one evening many years later in the Pompeian pool of my Nob Hill establishment.

"Bugs Baer and I were in San Francisco for a damn national political convention," Fowler said, "and we were bored to our umbilici. Liquor was scarce, females were political, and we'd been chicken cacciatored to death in every Italian restaurant in town. We yearned for something worthy of a town that is constantly quoting itself as The City That Knows How. Knows how to what? Operate cable cars? A dubious talent.

"So one of us—could have been me—commented that there was more hospitality in the outhouse of any New England farmhouse than in the entire city of San Francisco, with Oakland and Milpitas thrown in. This statement got to Rolph, and he came to investigate. He collected us, our confederates and accomplices and took us out to his home.

"Here he wined and dined us with food that still wets my tongue when I think of it ten years later; poured illegal but authentic liquor into us—until I, at least, was ready for a two weeks' cure. Then he asked us if there was anything else that our hearts desired.

"Baer said that his heart held an 'unfulfilled' desire. 'You couldn't scare up a cockfight, could you?' says Baer.

"The Mayor didn't hesitate a moment. He left the room, went out into his backyard and within five minutes he returned with two paranoid-looking roosters. Right there, in his living room and on a Persian rug that could not have been the same afterwards, we witnessed the greatest cockfight I've ever seen in my life. I lost ten dollars to the Chief of Police on the bird with the black wing feathers. And I still think the whole thing was rigged."

Well, that was the way Fowler told it to me, and that's the kind of man Rolph was. I remember him vividly in that lace-curtained, oaf-filled parlor so many years ago.

"So you're Sally Stanford," he said. "You're a pretty one."

I've got to admit that I was. I weighed a scant 110 pounds, I had chestnut hair and was wearing a stunning suit in two shades of blue with real ostrich feathers on my hat. I looked all right. Rolph said so and started negotiations. I smiled and pointed out demurely that I was the madam, not the merchandise. He was obviously disappointed, and looking back, I know I should have sampled a little for myself.

He asked me into his office. He inquired into the business thoroughly and gave me some fatherly advice about running a good, wholesome enterprise.

"Keep them clean and pretty, Sally!" was the gist of it. "And don't ever lose your class. Do things with class and style, and you'll always have the respect even of those who are against you, even the Bible-bangers. But avoid the bums and the crumbs of any business; stick to the top layer, and never, never below your class."

Well, this was the beginning of a long and fine friendship and maybe a lot more things of greater importance in my life. He did me many kindnesses, and I liked to think that I was, from time to time, able to even up the score a little. I know that my staff and I voted for him from dawn to daylight, whenever he ran. Even today, a generation later, his picture hangs in a hallowed place in my restaurant in Sausalito. Right over the cash register!

One time, when he had ducked his driver for a while, he called me from the grill at the Whitcomb Hotel, an old hangout of his, and suggested I drop over. We had a houseful, but I decided to let love reign without me for a while.

Jimmy was feeling pretty low and hung over. His moustache, which was snow-white against his baby-pink face, drooped and lacked its usual alert smartness. Even the carnation was wilted.

It seems his wife, Annie, had put private detectives on him and she'd gotten her money's worth. She sent a copy of the gumshoe's report to Jimmy's political adviser, Gavin MacNab. Something had to be done, she said, or their candidate for Governor in the next election might be a bachelor. Rolph had just left MacNab and Tim Reardon, another political boss and powerful labor leader.

They'd read the report to him. It told how the Mayor was called for at 9:30 A.M., at City Hall, by a blonde who took him to a hotel on Market Street where they'd dallied until eleven. At noon, he'd lunched with a brunette in an upstairs room at Jack's Restaurant where there were beds for the fatigued as well as food for the hungry. At 3:30 P.M., the Mayor had met another blonde with whom he had repaired to the Golden West Hotel to rest up until 6:30; which, as everyone in San Francisco knows, is time to start the cocktail route. This was more or less the mandatory itinerary which started at the House of Shields opposite the Palace Hotel and meandered down Montgomery Street, winding up at Camille's, across from the District Attorney's old office.

This trip the Mayor negotiated on the arm of a fourth female, color of hair unspecified in the report, probably because of the onset of darkness. Mrs. Rolph looked upon all this as a gross breach of Mr. Rolph's duty to the taxpayers, of whom she was Number One.

Rolph said that bosses MacNab and Reardon were thunderstruck by the length, breadth and complexity of their candidate's activities. MacNab had the only reaction worth remembering. He turned to Reardon and said in a broad Scottish accent, "This mon is a wastin' his God-given gifts taking any time out at all frrrrrom dooties such as these just to perforrrrm as Mayorrrr."

We chuckled over this. Then we discussed the enigma of women who are willing to pull the house down rather than see their man stray from the hearth's fires.

When next I saw Sunny Jim, he'd been elected Governor of California. He had invited me to Sacramento to see him and I went. He took time out from interviewing the Very Large Shots in the waiting room to call me into his office, talk with me, and discuss my problems, which were few at that time. He then showed me through his collections of photographs of earlier San Francisco.

When he died, I closed the business for the day and sent the largest floral display I could find, putting no card with it. I didn't want to blow his class.

My salad days were big enough, but they'd been short of the right kind of dressing. I've always liked smart, attractive clothes. And now, with all my geese laying golden eggs the whole night through, the busy little dears, I could dress and become accustomed to the high style.

Flamboyant clothes, the stereotype of a madam, never attracted me. Really fine dresses, hats and furs do more for my morale than Spanish fly does for the bull. Soon I was attracting more attention for my appearance than for my profession. I still like to make an entrance. I think every woman does. Diamonds, I go for. Today I wear them constantly. It comforts me to see the pretty things glittering away at the world, and besides, I could always hock them in my old age if things got rough. (You never know when that problem might pop up its ugly head as you move on in life.) On my ranch now they set off my cotton blouses and blue jeans.

In those beginning days, they were a great source of morale and far more stable in value than the Treasury Department's green stationery and for that matter, now that our dollar bills have had that *Payable in Silver Upon Demand* taken off forever, they have become even *more* stable than ever.

I began to get around socially a little more. I usually took along several of my prettiest girls. It was good advertising.

I met most of the colleagues in the business. What a wonderful set of women these were. I say with utmost sincerity that this is probably the most mutually loyal set of females in the world. We got and gave help when it was needed. We closed our ranks against the foe and made sure that no one used one of us against the other. All warnings, rumors and chunks of useful information were passed around to one and all.

They were a colorful crew. There is no point in listing names, for their stories have been told and retold in other books. Each had a specialty. One round butterball of a madam, who'd be rolling still had she ever fallen down, made her place at Sixth and Minna famous by allowing the customer another round with a young lady when the first tryst was unsatisfactory, her slogan being, "If at first you don't succeed, come come again."

And there was poor Lorraine Fontaine, found dead one night in her empty girl-less house, the faculty and student body having fled when she passed away. Understandably, no one wanted to indulge in lengthy conversations with investigating local authorities.

There was "Immaculate Maggie," so called by the newspapermen because she retired after twenty years as a madam without ever having had a single pinch (a phenomenon more incredible than the Indian rope trick). There was Marie—with a complicated French name that I can't recall—whose place was over a tire store at 620 Van Ness Avenue. A huge sign hung over her door reading: TIME TO RETIRE.

One or two in the group actually looked like madams. Most looked more like young society matrons. Of them all, I liked Mabel Malotte best. Mabel was a pro, a wonderful little woman. She had more class in her little finger than all of the people who finally cooperated in her crucifixion, including her most trusted friends.

For many years Mabel staged a high-voltage superclad love affair with a handsome policeman. This man was supposed to be able to take care of matters. Theirs was a Frankie and Johnnie affair, the flame of passion was unquenchable, etc. He was looking the other way, however, when night fell for Mabel.

I'm always reminded, when I hear of tales concerning "love undying," of Roy Brenner. Roy was a Mission mobster, a professional skull cracker who shot numerous holes through two women when they tried to break up his relationship with the sixteen-year-old daughter of one of them. The women made the morgue; Roy made the bucket. He gave the cops a very touching reply when asked why he did it. "Well, you know what love is," he said demurely.

Anyway, Mabel also handled her trouble badly when it came her way. She was sentenced to Corona for perjury and other offenses. Uncle Sam was waiting for her when she came out with a whole mess of other trouble, effective the day of her release. I kept in touch with her and we planned ways for her to fight off the nightmare and come back to some sort of life. Then she got cancer. But Mabel fought as she had always fought and managed to stay alive until her release.

God only knows what the prison did or did not do for Mabel, but she collapsed in the Greyhound Bus Terminal while trying to reach the Ladies' Room. She returned to San Francisco much later than expected. She was a shell of a woman. I remember thinking, If this woman is an example of the care being given cancer victims in prisons, God help us all.

She was admitted to the same hospital I was staying at in an attempt to recover completely from the coronary heart attack that floored me in December of 1958. She was on the same floor with me at Polyclinic Hospital on Pine Street, and regardless of the orders of my doctors, I wasn't going to be away from her side more than I had to. Not now when she needed someone more than at any time in her life. In the wee hours of the morning I would slip down the hall and into Mabel's room. She told me of many things and opened my eyes to things even I, with all my background, still found difficult to believe true.

She told me how her attorneys had never even called her in prison and how they had taken all of her money, in cash at that. She was terribly disillusioned by it all.

She told me again about her marriage to Sir Albert Hay Malotte, the man who wrote the song "The Lord's Prayer"—hence the name Malotte.

Finally, she asked me if I remembered a pact we had made many years ago, that if one of us should pass away, one before the other, the remaining one would see to it that no buzzing flies would be around our caskets and that the one to go would be buried from Halsteads on Sutter Street, an organization that does everything with a great deal of style and gentility and personal attention.

I promised her that I would take care of the details if anything should happen.

On the day before Christmas in 1958, her private nurse, a wonderful little English girl named Jones, tiptoed into my room and quietly told me that my friend Mabel was dead. Even knowing that it was to come, it was a shock. I immediately reached for the telephone and called Halsted's. I told them to pick up Mabel's remains and they said they had already had those orders and had picked up the remains early that morning.

Mabel, who embraced Catholicism, was buried from Old St. Mary's Cathedral, so I called Art Bell, my dear friend who owns the Sheridan-Bell Florists in Maiden Lane, and asked him to send a large spray of Mabel's favorite flowers, white orchids. I could not go, but Art Bell personally pinned the corsage on her shroud.

One ironic touch. Mabel had left all of her estate to her undying lover Victor Herbert, who wasn't around when Lady Luck walked out on his sweetheart. Victor Herbert wasn't around either when the money was counted out. He had died just thirteen days before Mabel. And it became clear to me that we're all hooked together in the pattern of destiny, in one way or another.

Like I always say, if you sit long enough by the crack of the door, you'll see your enemy go by in a hearse.

Six

A SILLY, gabby woman killed the Tenderloin and started San Francisco's night life on its way to limbo. It was 1940. This dame had less sense than a doorknob. Oh, yes, a lot of things happened between the original daffy act with which she started the bomb rolling and the final explosion that closed the town, but she was the one who started it, gentle readers, she was the one.

For us in the Tenderloin, things were moving well, depression or no depression. War, depression and trouble have always boomed the sin-for-sale business. My place was far better than most, but I was still just one of many. And my compulsive drive to be out in front was pushing me not to be a madam, but to be THE madam. Then it was that Princess Campbell came to town, and soon I had a mess of new fish to fry.

Princess Alice Kamokila Campbell was the wealthy daughter of a Hawaiian sugar planter named Campbell, by an allegedly bona fide princess (Knako variety) named Kuaihelana, and one easily impressed reporter described her as "exotic." Fine feathers make fine birds. She had the wherewithal to buy them and any woman will tell you what a little loot will do for your feathers.

The Lady of the House

This daffy twist arrived in San Francisco with a crockful of money. She had an urge to star in her own nightclub and a son named Pineapple McFarland (so help me God). She opened an establishment in the basement of a reformed Methodist Church at Bush and Jones streets. She called it the Club Kamokila. Before the varnish was thoroughly dry on her bar, this improbable female called the Police Department and asked to be connected with the man who collected the protection money!

The flabbergasted cop on the other end of the line was completely shook up, not knowing whether he was dealing with a trap or a nut or routine business. He referred the call to Chief William J. Quinn. That's when the mustard hit the fan. The Kamokila was raided and put on page one of all newspapers for a while. The princess made a lot of statements about having paid cops, was invited to tell the Grand Jury about it, agreed to do so, refused to do so, then hired attorney Jake Ehrlich to extract her from the jackpot.

Immaculate Jake, one of the town's top attorneys, eventually got the woman off the hook. She had caused panic in a lot of extremely delicate places. She was fond of issuing statements to the press and some of them were incendiary bombs. In one she really pinned the tail on the donkey.

"When a community is not courageous, it must expect vice and corruption. When one has to pay for respectability it is not fair. Let all of us good and patriotic citizens get together and clean up the city." Having thus tossed the dirt in the punch bowl and having buggered up the protection system on a long fuse, the princess packed up her hula skirts and went back to Hawaii. If there's any justice at all, she probably fell into a volcano. But then, she'd probably buy her way out.

I've mentioned my warning sixth sense; call it intuition, ESP, or a woman's whim, but it is the voice I always heed. It was now reacting like a five-alarm fire in my head. The princess was off page one. The town was filled with talk about protection. My personal warning system told me there would be a big shake-up and many changes. I had never paid off. I don't believe in it, but you don't make friends with "the protection" by with-holding your dues. I talked with everyone who might have a line on the action. My newspaper friends, including Harry Lerner, an ace investigative reporter who knew the town inside out, and everyone else on the party line, were of the opinion that San Francisco faced the end of a wide-open town as we'd known it. Bankruptcy of the McDonoughs' power was in the cards.

It seemed that everyone was checking on someone. A swivel-tongued employee of the Bureau of Internal Revenue told a luncheon club in suburban Mill Valley that a San Francisco police captain was being checked out on the suspicion of having piggy-banked over a hundred thousand dollars from his annual salary of about seven thousand. A cute trick if you can do it.

It was also rumored that certain madams were being investigated for having attempted to list graft payoffs as business expenses. Harvey Wing, a particularly sharp newspaperman, pounced eagerly on these incidents. We were off to the races again with PROTECTION all over page one once more and no rest for the wicked.

The Grand Jury got into the act, and, motivated by one Princess Blabbermouth from Hawaii, accepted an idea of hers and got an appropriation to investigate corruption. It was rumored a peerless professional peeper would be imported for the job.

A matter of days later I was shopping for towels at Sixth and Mission streets (an item vital to the love business) when I ran into a young policeman friend of mine standing next to two other old friends of mine: Billy John, who couldn't resist stealing sunglasses from drugstores, and a paddy wagon.

Billy John had been pinched this time for assault with a deadly weapon, a swan. Billy John had swiped the swan at Stow

Lake in Golden Gate Park. He had a gourmet type friend who believed a dash of swan was what was needed for his specialty, Italian polenta. On his way to his friend's kitchen, Billy John met a former wife of his. And in the electric agitation of two hostile souls airing a beef, Billy John clobbered her with the swan. Billy John did things with a flair.

After cueing me in with the details of Billy John's ornithological mishap, my policeman friend lowered his voice and told me to watch out for a great big, large-shouldered, square-jawed joker who would probably call by and ask questions other than those a madam expects from a client. That was the first time I heard the name Atherton—a name that was to rock the town before long.

Several days later another policeman by the name of Frank Lucey came by the house one afternoon at breakfast time. He often dropped by for coffee and occasionally knew the correct score. Lucey got right to the point:

"You're going to have to close, Sally. It might even be a good idea to take a little vacation, you and the girls. Reno's very nice this time of year."

"You mean just my place?"

"Hell, no! Everyone. Everyone this side of the dry goods business. The heat is on."

And then he told me the Grand Jury had hired Edwin Atherton, a former FBI man turned professional peeper. A plague of graduate gumshoes had descended on the city like a flock of locusts. They were determined to trace the origin of every cop's dollar not listed on his civil service paycheck. A few telephone calls to well-connected friends of mine confirmed this prediction. I decided to stop answering doorbells, devote my time to my thesis, and explain it to the girls.

The ladies were quite upset.

It was just before the holidays and unless they did a lot of

Christmas-loving, they weren't going to do much Christmas shopping. I told them better December on a diet than June in the jug, and they rushed to their digs to break the sad news to their respective "Old Men." Pimps, being highly sensitive to female idleness, could be heard wailing all over the Tenderloin.

Long before the former G-man came out with his now famous Atherton Report, things began to go into a tailspin. Some cops who depended more upon The Action than upon the city for their income were upset, demoralized at the heretofore omnipotent McDonoughs for not having prevented such a revolting development. Their allegiance and respect were beginning to falter.

My colleagues, on the other hand, were just plain sore. Their dues had been paid in advance, and they were getting neither protection rebates nor words of sympathy as they turned away eager customers who might produce a badge and a subpoena from their pocket. It was all very hard on the central nervous system. My dues were not paid.

When the report finally came out, it turned out to be a diner on wheels with knobs and spangles. It was seventy pages long. It named and located every joint in town, every girl on every staff, plus her measurements, and her preference in disinfectants. Some very interesting statements were made about finances of a great number of police officers (some of them of very high rank, the poor dears), and it told the entire story of the McDonough Brothers' operation.

And then, one bright afternoon, the old nervous system really had a jolt.

It was too early in the day for business. None of the girls had shown up yet. I was counting the receipts from the night before, and Gloria, the basic black maid of the moment, was restoring order and dignity to the towel supply. I was checking the records I kept: the initials of the girls, the check marks that tallied their scores, the first names of some public servants, and other miscellaneous items. The doorbell rang and trouble had his thumb on the button—literally, as it turned out.

Gloria answered the door, took a peep through the Judas hole, came back looking dubious.

"This man I ain't never seen before. He say he have friend."

My premonition warning sounded loud and clear. Some of the money I was counting I stuffed into the bottom of a smoking stand, and those records that wouldn't fit into my bra I put under a cushion on the settee. Then I went to the peephole and looked out at a "great big, large-shouldered, square-jawed joker," and I knew I was nose to nose with brother Atherton. We smiled at each other like it was love at first sight and he asked, "Is the lady of the house in?"

"Come in, come in," I said, opening the door. "I don't know why my cleaning woman hesitated for a moment, except that there are so many rapists in the region. What are you selling? Kitchenware?"

He good-naturedly denied being a salesman and I ushered him into the parlor and unhappily watched him sit on the records.

"No, Miss Stanford," he said, and he thrust out his big he-man jaw. "You are far too smart a woman for me to fence with. I'm Mr. Atherton, the investigator."

He handed me a card upon which were his picture and credentials. I looked at it like it was the Dead Sea Scrolls.

"Fancy that," I said, in obvious awe. "Why in the world would you be wanting to talk to the proprietor of a quiet little place for rented rooms, like me?"

"Come on, Sally!" he broke in, laughing gaily as if we had had our little joke and now it was time to get on with the real stuff. "Everyone knows that you run a good, clean, sensible house of prostitution, and that you are respected in the business.

The Lady of the House

We can talk, Sally! I'm not interested in giving you a bad time."

The melody is always the same, and I knew these lyrics by heart. The next remarks would be to the effect that he was after only the people who were exploiting me, not just the "underlings" but the "higher-ups." Nothing would happen to me, except that when the hassle was over, I might have to go to work in a laundry, folding sheets.

"Mr. Atherman—" I said.

"Atherton, Atherton," he broke in, displaying the card again.

"Mr. Atherton, I haven't the slightest idea why you're here. I rent rooms. I go to church Sundays. I listen to *One Man's Family* on the radio. It isn't much of a life, but it's better than some I know of, Mr. Atherman."

"Atherton. I wish you would try to trust me, Sally. I . . ."

"The last man I trusted went down the rear fire escape with his bags, all but one. The one he left me holding. Six weeks' rent I trusted him for. Please crush out your cigarette real well before dropping it into that smoking stand. I'm deadly afraid of fires."

Just then, Gloria came through the room with about ninety towels over her arm, humming away as happily as a damn bumblebee in a fuchsia bed. I could've killed her! Atherton bug-eyed the towels.

"We take a lot of baths," I said, wondering if, like the princess on the pea, his posterior was sensitive to the bulge under the cushion upon which he was sitting.

"And it has been nice speaking with you. I'll give a lot of thought about what you've said. If I see anything suspicious happening in the neighborhood, I'll just give you a call, Mr. Atherstein, and—"

"Atherton, Atherton," he said, getting up and starting for the door, and he said, "Don't call us; we'll call you."

And he did, the son of a bitch. He called all our hands, had an ace-high straight and nearly took the pot.

The cows had come home and anyone with sense enough to pour uric acid out of a boot could see that nothing short of Divine Intervention could save the McDonough Brothers' system of protection. Atherton didn't pull any punches in his statements. I got the message loud and clear, though his grammar seemed a little strange to little old third-grade graduated madam, me.

The Atherton Report was pretty hot chile. Policemen, lieutenants, and other characters were indicted for bribery. Most of them quickly showed their loss of faith in the attorneys the Organization had. Some retained Jake "the Master" Ehrlich.

Other cops, quick like frightened rabbits, took their retirement and disappeared. Still others became sick and went on long leaves. The odds were good indeed that their illnesses, possibly psychosomatic, were the real McCoy. I know I felt under the weather myself, and one unfortunate policeman shot his wife and his mother-in-law just before he blew himself into eternity.

Most of the embattled lads doggedly shook their heads and swore it wasn't so. Many flannel-mouthed Micks, who'd arrived barefoot from Ireland a few years previously, piously called upon "the Hawley Vargin" to witness the truth of their claims that they'd saved their thousands in lucky bets on horses and the parish hall wheels of chance. One ostrich-minded captain was utterly flabbergasted when the investigators pulled $25,000 out of his woodshed.

"Well, wouldn't that amaze you?" he said, openmouthed. "Some evil person must have hid it there."

His solution to the issue was that the mysterious money should be put back in the woodshed, and the area staked out nights so as to catch the villain when he came back for his ill-gotten twenty-five thousand.

A great number of the suspected made the mistake of trusting their banks with the mistaken idea that a deposit account was a holy trust. But no one had estimated Atherton sufficiently. He went into court and made it crystal-clear that unless the bankers came through with the information he wanted, he would and could back a truck against their front doors and take all their records. And at his leisure sift through them. The banks got the idea fast. The depositors' right to privacy became public knowledge.

At about this time, Harry Lerner's news-hawking uncovered sensational involvements between the McDonough Brothers and higher-ups, including a $2,500 loan to Matt Brady, the District Attorney at the time, from the Brothers (who right now were *plenty* Grimm). All of which was published by the *Chronicle* and later confirmed by the Atherton Report. I decided to protect myself and keep my eggs in many baskets.

I had working establishments at 837 Geary Street, 1526 Franklin, 929 Bush (called Lysol Alley in those days; an expression went around something to the effect, "Are you married or do you live on Lysol Alley?" Real funny stuff *then*), and an Oriental establishment at 1224 Stockton Street in Chinatown. I figured it would take the whole police force and half the privates from the Presidio to close all my shops at one time.

My place on Taylor Street was adjacent to the Japanese Consulate. One evening three young ladies found themselves receiving an unexpected delegation of policemen. While the boys in blue were sounding out the maid, the three girls departed by the rear fire escape and made it safely into the back of the Consulate. There they told a bowing Japanese gentleman that they had just escaped the unpleasant attention of a group of rapists.

The Lady of the House

The Oriental gentleman must have been a descendant of a Samurai for he offered personally to punish the rapists. He summoned a cab, escorted the ladies into it, and sped them on their way. The bewildered police watched this action, goggle-eyed, from a window in the raided premises, painfully unsure of just how immune diplomatic immunity could get.

My Chinatown house was vivid proof that "East is East and West is West, and never the twain shall meet" is just a lot of chow mein. The twain met more regularly and profitably there than in any of the 580 houses that were reported to exist in San Francisco. I had one thing going which no one else in the business could lay claim to.

The message SALLY'S GOT A NEW GIRL was printed in Chinese characters and posted on every telephone pole and building all over Chinatown, and no one read it but the wily Oriental. Curiously enough, no one ever mentioned this item to the boys with the stars. Hear no evil, see no evil, speak no evil was, I guess, translated from Confucius. And in gratitude, once a month, all proceeds of this house were dedicated to the relief of the starving in China. And the customers, eager to help their countrymen, filled many a pillowcase with money. Eager to spread the news, many an excited Oriental gentleman, or young buck, would run down the street yelling, "One a dozen, two a dozen [pidgin English for 1224] gotta new girl." And customers would suddenly line up in the streets clear down to Broadway, a block away.

But the wheel had a way of coming off our wagon from time to time. One night the hostess in charge phoned to say that the landlord, a local attorney, had shown up and was complicating business by knocking on doors at the wrong moments. Orientals may bathe in public, but they draw the line at other kinds of exposure. It wasn't that the landlord wanted to interrupt what was going on, nor did he care. He just wanted more rent, but he picked a hell of a time to talk about it.

I quickly gathered a posse of associates and we taxied to Chinatown. Looking back on the incident and considering that this nosey self-appointed guardian of private property was poaching on my domain, I still believe that I handled the matter with delicacy, restraint and diplomacy.

Keeping my solemn vow to myself, never to be broke again, my blood-pressure rage and adrenaline output increased with compound interest whenever anyone interfered with my income. I arrived with my companions at about 11:30 P.M. The landlord regarded us as intruders; he reported to the papers that he gently closed the door in the faces of my companions and me. Not accustomed to having the door of my own house shut in my own face, I kicked it in—it was a glass door. I announced my intention of tearing him apart and proceeded to carry out my promise. He left the premises rapidly. We took the soiled linen (mostly pillowcases stuffed with money) as though it were laundry, and divided the spoils, sending an extra token for the distressed in China.

Personally, I never met a white slave in my life—not a female one, that is. If captive females were sold, drugged, or slugged into prostitution, I never knew a case. A far more common thing (and a continual nuisance) was the arrival at my various front doors of numberless who wanted work. Especially they wanted me for their employer. Most of them were clearly unfitted, being either dull, too plain, too young, or completely without experience. Most of them I sent on their way with advice to keep out of the business; the desperate and hungry I gave a piece of change. The nonprofessionals I had no use for. They ruined the business in the same fashion as an untrained, inexperienced court reporter would mess up the records. A good girl needs a lot more than standard equipment.

It was quite amazing the kind of variety of females who rang my front bells hunting jobs. Starving jobless dames? Forget it. The greatest number of candidates were women who just wanted to be prostitutes. They weren't driven to it. They didn't have to. They wanted to have intercourse with men for money, and for many the first item was more important than the second.

Some, of course, were just plain lazy. Others had the strange idea that any activity illicit in nature was glamorous.

Obviously a large slice of the applicants were neurotic. Otherwise, scared twists whose marriages or love affairs had soured were often trying to get back at their men in some nutty fashion. A few tried to turn themselves out as a means of getting back at their families, most particularly at their fathers. A lot is to be said about the affection that prostitutes have for their fathers. Psychiatrists play the variations on the theme of mother-hate. It's their favorite tune.

The common-garden variety of nymphomaniac is everywhere. On the other hand, there are a lot of plain and lonely girls whose reasons for showing up have more to do with loneliness than the desire to become glamorous queens of the red-light district. It's certainly a helluva note when the desperate need for affection drives an unattractive girl to try a racket for which she is entirely unsuited in order to get a little intimate attention from men.

Togetherness in a bargain basement. Every size, shape, color and variety of dope addict wants in the profession. The reasons are simple and practical. The narcotic's habit is expensive, easily costing fifty to seventy-five dollars a day. Outside of professional crime or amazing luck at Bingo, is there any other job that can support a nasty habit like that? I had learned years ago to recognize hopheads immediately. They are all messed up and they foul up the business and keep you in trouble constantly.

I never knowingly put one to work.

Most of them had their own habit to support plus that of their pimp.

One slipped by me for a few days, a beautiful, charming and educated girl whose youthful freshness would have deceived the narcotics bureau of the FBI. She took her money and I never saw her again. I learned the bitter truth when the newspapers published her picture under a different name. She had been found dead from an overdose of heroin in the hills back of Hayward, California. Her boyfriend later admitted to the crime.

Oddities we had aplenty. A University of Washington grad with a master's degree wanted to write a book. She gathered her material in the field, or rather in the feathers. One twist fondly thought she had developed some new ways to do old things and was going to revolutionize the business.

And one, believe it or not—and this is the honest-to-God truth, so help me Kinsey—actually got by me and came to work. And I discovered she didn't know what her date wanted to do when she took him up to the bedroom! Horrified at the businesslike way in which her client prepared to go into action, she excused herself, came to me, and told me she was not prepared to go quite that far. This story has an incredible but equally true payoff. With my consent (I must have been so stunned I didn't know what I was doing), she went back to the man and charmed the poor flabbergasted soul out of the notion of sex and into a willingness to take her out dancing. It was *his* last evening with us, and it was *her* last night as well.

I said I'd never seen a woman sold, but once I saw a man sold and with rather interesting consequences. A colleague of mine, who disappeared from the scene in San Francisco, once had a strapping young Italian friend named John.

The Lady of the House

John was like one of those characters in the afterpart of the Before-and-After Vic Tanny advertisements. He was a combination of Steve Reeves and Cassius Clay. He didn't have a pretzel to his name, and his profession appeared to be easing the chair under the madam's rear in expensive restaurants. That and other things a strong man can do for a weak woman.

This madam was walking her John on Geary Street one day when she ran into a French madam from Vallejo, a town up-Bay from San Francisco where a madam has her hands full. In those days the whole Navy lived in or visited Vallejo.

The French know what they want when they see it, so I'm told. And a deal was made. John and two thousand dollars exchanged hands. A good man may be hard to find, but two thousand dollars isn't exactly carfare to the zoo. The bargain was sealed. Unfortunately, the Immigration Department later discovered that the French lady was here illegally. They deported her to La Belle France where she promptly joined her ancestors.

The purchased boyfriend inherited everything, and the moral to this parable is: there is nothing wrong with white slavery—if you happen to be a man.

It only takes one mistake to louse up the whole game, and eight teen-aged boys damn near closed every brothel in San Francisco. This episode has been covered by other books of this period, and it's true that I had turned away this octet of teen-aged brats a short while before they gained entrance and were caught in another house. The madam was wearing a red dress when the police arrived. All the papers called her "The Lady in Red." The judges and public were so upset over the callow curiosity of some socially prominent kids that somebody had to pay the bill. I considered a slow boat to Shanghai and opening a house as a young, sober, hard-working madam with a taste for chow mein. I have never seen The Lady in Red since, and she served her time and disappeared—that was Dolly Fine, a helluva wonderful gal.

The Tenderloin began to fall apart. Vacant stores pock-marked the streets. Neon signs went out over cafés. and it was then that I decided I'd had it.

I remembered what Sunny Jim Rolph had told me so many years before: "Do everything with class and style." Avoid the crumbs and bums and stick to the top layer. I knew where I was going. I was going after the class, the carriage trade.

There was logic involved. If you were going into the shoplifting business, you'd hardly try Woolworth's when Tiffany's was within walking distance. And this was the reason for abandoning the plebeian lowland section of San Francisco for Nob Hill, Russian Hill and Pacific Heights where the carpets are thicker, the checks larger, and the birds sing sweetly all the day.

Seven

THE house was no castle in Spain. Built in 1900, it was a palace. Number 1001 Vallejo Street, still a San Francisco showplace, was built by Robert Hanford for his fourth wife, Helen Maud McCann, and the architects and contractors had been given carte blanche. I don't know about Robert's taste in female beauty, but I know we had similar tastes in the house, because when I graduated from the Russian Hill château I moved into another house he built on Nob Hill for still another woman. This was the place at 1144 Pine Street where much of this story takes place. Both houses were spectacular. And both were fortresses. It was impossible for anyone to get into either of them unless we wanted to open the doors.

Let's talk about sex.

I've always believed that sex is the simplest and most fundamental thing in nature. Attraction, fertilization, and conception; the flower opens to spill its perfume and display its most glorious colors to attract pollen-bearing insects and fulfill its need. Birds don their gayest plumage and perform their rhythmic dances to attract mates. It is basic.

The Lady of the House

Even a noncultured, uncouth teen-aged ruffian follows the pattern. He may douse himself with thick-smelling hair goo and wash his ears, but most always he finds a lovers' lane high on a hill with a magnificent view as the place to try out his fumbling studies in comparative anatomy. Beauty is an essential part of it.

I was determined to have the most beautiful, elegant, grand temple of love. I think I made it, and so do a lot of others. I appealed to every taste. Every room and every floor was different. One whole floor was designed and decorated as an exclusive hunting lodge. The Pompeian Court with its fountain, fireplace and pools has been described as breath-taking. Oriental rooms, Italian and French Provincial, Venetian Renaissance, were decorated with the finest antiques, glorious and plush draperies and carpets. My girls were equally beautiful, refined charmers. Soft music was piped throughout. Food, prepared exquisitely and served with fabulous vintage wines, was the order of the day. And the customers loved it.

At the new place we were concerned only with the kind of men who were not concerned with price tags. Thirty to fifty dollars was average for a half hour of a girl's time. Girls who went out got fifty dollars an hour, whether it was for dinner, dancing, or horizontal exercise. Many guests paid from two hundred fifty to five hundred dollars for hospitality. Five-hundred-dollar tabs for entertainment, including liquor and food, were not uncommon.

For the large tabs my gentlemen guests got large quality.

When the gentlemen arrived, they were greeted by a host or hostess who satisfied themselves that the guests were neither policemen nor paupers. Having been escorted through a series of iron gates and locked doors into a huge drawing room, they were met by fashionably dressed young ladies who came and went like guests at a house party. Wong Hee, my new Chinese butler (as former lottery ticket peddler, he knew every cop in the Tenderloin), served the drinks. The guests were always introduced to the girls as Mr. Jones, Mr. Green, Mr. Smith or Mr. Charles Brown. (I've met a lot of Charlie Browns since then.)

The furniture was antique, authentic and tastefully chosen. The music was so skillfully unobtrusive that I've often wondered how much Muzak learned from me. The conversation was as good as any that went on in the neighborhood—better, probably. I never allowed a girl to tell a dirty story because I found that the kind of men who now came to my place resented such stories from the lips of a woman. Men sometimes are excited by raw remarks from women they regard as nice. But they are even more excited by prim conversation from women who are supposed to be bad.

As time went on, not all of those who frequented my drawing room came there for sex. Some were well-known politicians, actors, and financiers (though still addressed as Smith, Jones, Green or Brown). They came just for the drinks, the company, or to see me; no one really knew for sure when or if anything else took place. No client was ever touted on or urged to get off the dime and make for the beds. When he was ready to make his choice, he chose his date, negotiated with the host and disappeared with the lady. No girl ever handled anything as sordid as money. And as for me, unless some kind of a crisis arose I was as removed from any of the surface amenities of prostitution as if I were a housemother at Vassar.

Behind the scenes I worked to make this the most exclusive rendezvous for lovers on earth. I decorated the rooms with the finest antiques. I was particularly interested in furniture with a history or a name associated with it. In one of the better rooms, I had the personal bed of Elsie DeWolfe whom you may remember as Lady Mendl. Sheets and bedding were the best, and every bathroom was stocked with any and all of the articles that my guests could desire.

The Lady of the House

I chose the girls with equal care. Nearly all were from out of town. Former show girls, models, and a large number of refugees from the motion picture colony decorated the salons. A few were disgusted divorcees. In no time at all I had a waiting list longer than the Junior League. No society merchant was more meticulous about his wares than I was about mine. Each candidate had the services of my medical doctor, my hairdresser and dressmaker. I suggested petticoats with plenty of lace and ribbons, and one of the hosts taught the girls ballet when business was slow.

No astronaut ever got a more thorough briefing than I gave a girl new to the house. They were to lead circumspect lives, avoid associating with each other away from the business, and pass up all after-hours joints and other off-color spots where they might be pinched or even seen by cruising plainclothesmen. They were to avoid seeing or talking to customers away from the house, which might lead men to making unilateral agreements with the ladies—or even more revolting, getting it for free.

I warned them constantly against the eventual arrival of the inevitable pimp—the handsome bastard they would share their 4 A.M.'s with, their confidences, and their bank rolls. Each girl would solemnly assure me that she was too smart to take that route, but the advice rarely did any good. Sooner or later most would show up with a black eye and a request for an advance, and I'd know there was nothing to do but fork over the money.

So this was the house that Sally built. These were the girls that worked in the house that Sally built. I did my conniving, scheming, defensive best for them. They did their enticing, seductive, coquettish best for me, the little dears, and the house prospered. For their efforts I gave them 60 percent of the take. This was pretty damned generous, of course, but then they were a lovely set of girls and they contributed quite a bit to the success of the place, too.

Even gentlemen have some pretty daffy foibles, I learned as time went on, and as I began a guest list that would have pleased any society matron, particularly one with unmarried daughters. These guests of mine were the wealthiest big spenders of the town. Most of them came from the so-called "better classes." Some are still friends of mine.

Our problems were varied. For instance, one of the town's most eligible bachelors exhibited behavior that might have intrigued Dr. Freud. With him, it was weak kidneys. When in his cups, he would and did go in any available vase, coal bucket, umbrella stand, champagne cooler, or upended crate. And despite the fact that his tabs were high and his checks were good, he had his annoying moments.

Worst of all was the silent and unannounced nature of his responses to the call of nature. When the urge struck him while he was a little stoned, he would merely go to the nearest receptacle and my first warning would be the screams of the girls to the effect that "He's at it again." Or as in one lamentable and expensive case—the furious shouts of another gentleman guest whose brand-new hundred-dollar Stetson got the treatment. But even apprehended in midstream, he was a problem. It is very hard to turn a man off once he's turned on. When hell was raised with him about these departures from decorum, he would become momentarily contrite and use a kitchen or a bathroom sink for a while. For some strange reason, he couldn't be persuaded to move up, or down, to commodes.

Even in his sleep I couldn't trust him. It is said that in the Pine Street house, Anna Held had dallied with Hanford the lumber king. Her marble tub and an enormously handsome Chesterfield were there. I had upholstered the Chesterfield in a magnificent pink brocade. And our friend with the leaky plumbing had passed out on it after a few bottles of champagne. As the party wore on, we covered him up and left him to sleep it off.

The next morning, as soon as the banks were opened I cashed the checks given to me the night before, as was my habit. On my return to the house, I lifted the cover from our still sleeping faucet, only to discover he'd done it again. He was dyed bright pink from the nape of his neck to his heels. I still call him "Pinky" and when I need a few donations for a cause or favorite charity, I can call Pinky today and be assured of a donation. He married into one of San Francisco's most wealthy and social families, but even afterward he continued to visit me and my girls. The bride did not appreciate this loyalty and took to calling me up and demanding that I send him home. When politely told that he wasn't there, she would become abusive and threaten to have me raided. I've heard that on each anniversary she receives, among other presents, a gift-wrapped condom, and this annoys her, inasmuch as she ascribes this crude gesture to me—of all persons. I have neither time nor condoms to waste.

Another sometimes difficult guest who, in time, married into a wealthy and social sugar clan—let's call him Carl. Carl was a doll and the girls all loved him dearly. Unfortunately he had a weakness, when in his cups, of forgetting to pay his bill.

For him I had a special house rule. I had the host pick up his shoes and hide them early in each visit. One night when Carl was present there was a wild false alarm of a raid following an unusually loud outcry from a set of frustrated cops who actually never got past the street door. With this confusion downstairs, the maid herded a scrambling assortment of men and girls out another door. Among them was Carl, who must have provided a conversation piece for a small, select group of San Franciscans during the week that followed as the man who went home on the California Street cable car barefooted.

One multimillionaire guest was bugged on toilet seat cleanliness, and we provided him with a small brush. He would watch the bathroom door and as each guest departed, he would pop in like a fussy little old maid and carefully scrub the seat.

Another would move into my place whenever he left or was left by one of his several wives. On one occasion he left home and hearth with significant finality by packing all of his personal effects—clothes, papers, books, golf clubs, in fact everything on earth that he valued—into a sedan. Then he headed for my place. He was completely stoned when he arrived. I put him to bed, alone. He forgot to tell me that he had parked his car in front or I'd have garaged it. Not only was the car gone next morning, it had disappeared forever. Every personal effect the poor man had was gone with it. He was so discouraged that he damn near became a permanent guest. It was a week before I could encourage him to the point where he would go out and start life all over again with the purchase of a new shirt.

Playboys sometimes faced the dawn with a feeling that the tab on last night's fun was a little high. Occasionally, some jokester would cancel payment on a check. Usually they brought their accounts up to date by the time the next urge for an evening of mirth, frivolity and feckless living struck them. With some, however, it got to be a contest of wills.

One tycoon, whose major purposes in life were to put his product between the earth and every human being, and to have nothing but good old girlie fun, was addicted to this corny game. Most often I could get to the bank before he woke up and stopped payment on last night's checks. However, occasionally he beat me to the draw. Being an American citizen and assured of my rights, naturally I sued the hell out of him. My playful and reluctant tycoon claimed that his physical condition at the time rendered him incapable of signing a check. He then proceeded to add insult to injury and alleged that a complete absence of compensation characterized his visit to my establishment. Obviously, he did sign the check and my attorney pointed out that if he could write his name, he would surely remember reacting to and appreciating the compensations available in a lively playpen like mine.

Just to spur his memory a bit concerning the events of the evening, I sent the young lady who had personally provided compensations, to his office to see him. Naturally, Caroline was inclined to be a little salty at the idea of having her professional reputation besmirched. I'm sure that her round little bottom must have scorched a semicircle in his waiting room chair.

The case was settled out of court, and the checks honored.

I restored his welcome a few days later when he sent me some jewelry as a gesture toward preserving his credit card and entree at my portals. I restored his welcome, but not his credit. And though he pleaded, for me the game was over; the love-for-a-signature days were ended for the dear old check-stopping playboy.

One of the pillars of society down the Peninsula from San Francisco was a regular and cherished guest. He devised a plan whereby to save his family's failing fortune and his business, which somehow had slid practically into bankruptcy. He brought with him an elderly gentleman, working on the premise that some excitement, fun and frivolity might soften the old lad up for a touch of fifty thousand or more. Well, we tried. We turned on everything. The colored lights played on the fountain in the Pompeian Court, the champagne flowed, and the girls were charming, lovely and delightful. And the old gentleman was amazed and a little aghast at the splendor of the place. He kept saying over and over, "I didn't know such a place existed," and would shake his head in wonderment, as a little child might at his first three-ring circus. In the small hours he agreed to help his friend and my customer and made out a check for $50,000. We all had a drink to celebrate the saving of the business, and the two gentlemen went to bed with a covey of lovelies.

The next morning over coffee the elderly gentleman complained bitterly that it was just too expensive, tipped each girl a dime and canceled his check. We never saw either of them again.

The word spread and we began to pick up a few exotics, and though we had the blue-blooded clientele with clean necks and money in the pocket, we also had problems. For one thing there were special requests, and the best way to describe them is to use a term the colored maids liked: "freakishness."

These lads were inventive. Some wanted to do it wearing grass skirts, or to the beat of a bass fiddle, with a poodle present, or hanging from the chandelier, and so on and on. So-called French love, multiple poon, ceiling mirrors, ostrich feathers, warm wet towels, were not enough. We went along with these caper clowns as far as we could, but the line was drawn when the super-perversions—sadism, masochism, pederasty, or other games bordering on mayhem—were requested.

Most of these lads came from very wealthy families and claimed their psychiatrists or therapists had said it would be good for them. Therapy and fun I'm all for, but I was running a wholesome-minded seraglio for gentlemen lechers. No more than three girls to a customer at any one time.

Most customers, actually, fell into one of several categories. There was the routine trick: He would drink a little, talk a little, make love a little, put on his clothes and go home. He might be there for a number of reasons, but curiously enough, he was rarely there because of his libido. Sex was usually a secondary reason with this gentleman. He was there because things were bad at home. He'd gotten hell from his wife. There were too many dirty dishes in the sink, or she was unfaithful, or worse yet, unpleasant.

Unhappy husbands fill everybody's house but their own. Men tell women like me things they wouldn't tell God, or their therapists, and certainly not their wives. I've listened to a lot of tales from men that came to my house apparently to have intercourse, but really just because they were lonely and unhappy. Wives of these men would be more amazed and angry and hurt by what was said about life at home than knowing about the casual thing that took place on the mattress.

Then there is the ashamed drunk, the kind of man who feels the proper place to take drunkenness is a house of prostitution. Here, he tells himself, he'll be appreciated. He isn't. He is seldom capable of doing what he came for. He is loud, argumentative, and practical-jokish at pay time, and unless such types were old and dear customers, I sent them away.

Then there's the gent, the patronizing character who regards himself as a Grand Seigneur mingling briefly with the unfortunate. This monkey takes up valuable bed space with some logical research: "Tell me, my dear, how did a beautiful thing like you ever become a . . . get into this line of work?" Some of my girls should have been writing fiction; they concocted some wonderful life histories for these yoyos, most of whom were male whores themselves supported by a wealthy wife or other source that did them no credit.

Lonely men all touched me, particularly bachelors who had spent the evening shaking dice at a bar and watched their pals go home to families, or who had been dinner guests at the suburban homes of married friends and somehow found it impossible

The Lady of the House

to return immediately to an empty apartment. They came regularly, which is significant of how regularly they were lonely. Most were really attractive men.

We got our quota of strange, intent, cold-eyed ones who were quietly but deeply mentally ill. Their illness became obvious after a few drinks and their dark desires came to the surface. Most were trying to prove to themselves that they were men. Never quite convinced deep inside themselves, they would bring their buddies with them and proceed to prove "There's nothing wrong with me, is there Joe?" We processed them and sent them on their way as quickly as possible and were seldom home if they returned.

And there were the youngsters, the college types and a little older and a little younger. To the rah-rah boys, it was less sex than a lark if they came in a group. There would be lots of skylarking and adolescent jokes about the wonderful thing they had just discovered. There was more bottom slapping and raucous laughing than I personally cared for. Single college boys were apt to be more dignified and purposeful; they were investigating manhood and proving to themselves that they were genuine, authentic males. The younger ones we got rid of on the first bounce.

I can still remember the innocent, cherubic face of a fourteen-year-old who thought he'd be welcome because his father—a local attorney—was, and because he had saved his allowance for ten weeks and had fifty dollars in his hot little hand. I walked him down to the corner and straightened him out on the way:

"If you ever ring my bell again until you can show me a driver's license which shows you to be of age, I'll personally kick hell out of you and call your father."

"Aw, I just want to see what's inside," he said.

"Just what I figured," I told him, remembering the eight so-

—❦ 111 ❧—

ciety brats who had sent my colleague, The Lady in Red, into
retirement. "You're just what I don't need, so go back to school
and grow up. So long, Sonny."

"So long, madam."

Loving thy neighbor is sometimes pretty hard to do, particularly when the jerk blows the whistle on you, and this is what
some of my pedigreed neighbors on Russian Hill began to do.
The house was best known as the old Verdier place, and the
neighbors were some of the wealthiest, socially prominent
people in the Bay area. One charming matron who had moved a
few doors from me, being completely unknown except for a
tremendous wealth, had just finished redecorating her new
home.

Feeling friendly and neighborly, she decided to give an
evening "At Home." She wanted to meet her neighbors and
show them her lovely new house. So she tucked little invitations
under each door, inviting the neighbors to drop by. I said to the
girls, "Well, let's go. It may be a lark." And so, as her party was
going full swing and the orchestra was playing soft music, we
arrived and were received royally.

Naturally, many of my guests were there, and with the wine
and the music and the laughter, some joker with a leaky mouth
dropped the word that Sally Stanford and her stable of fillies
were attracting most of the male guests. The hostess disappeared, and the party died of its own volition. The girls had a
ball; the men loved it; business boomed, and complaints of unspecified goings-on at the big house at the top of the hill flooded
the switchboard of the police station.

One day I received a visit from Captain Emmett Moore of
Central Station, a really nice guy, and he made it clear that he
was getting more and more telephone squawks. He felt that
some of them were going to the Chief, and perhaps higher.

The Lady of the House

I decided to move to another house in just as deluxe a district and set up camp where the neighbors had more to do than to peep through their draperies and put a stopwatch on the visits of my guests. Besides, the roof had begun to leak and there were complaints during the rainy season from those who didn't appreciate the sensuous delight of a trickle of water on a bare bottom.

So it was in 1941 that I bought the house at 1144 Pine Street. That was a wonderful place, and there I was to remain until November of 1949, when I left the business and became a legitimate square.

Had I designed it myself, the house could not have been more perfect. From the outside it was known as "The Fortress"; and on the inside it had been described as breathtaking, magnificent and unbelievable. Bob Hanford had built it for his third lover, the beautiful and talented Anna Held. It was said to have been designed by Stanford White, the famed New York architect who was killed at the old Madison Square Garden by Harry K. Thaw because of some nonarchitectural designs he carried out on his wife.

On the Pine Street side, this building was buttressed by a high stone wall of hand-hewn rock created by Chinese coolies of the early San Franciscan days. The same type of wall surrounds the famous Mark Hopkins Hotel. The only entry was through a huge wrought-iron gate which would have kept out a regiment of Marines. (Not that I would have barred their way had they come for the right purpose and bearing money.) Behind the iron gate was another one equally invulnerable to assault. This house was built on the site of the old Fair mansion and at the time the Fairs were building the Fairmont Hotel when the Fire came along.

Upstairs there was a lovely split-level living room the full width of the house. The fireplace would have stabled a quartet of Clydesdale horses. Adjoining the mammoth drawing room was the Pompeian Court, which held a marble pool where Anna Held, for whom the house was said to have been built, had supposedly taken her milk baths. This marble plunge would have held a helluva lot of milk, but that we never used. We held some very interesting social aquatic events, however.

Considering my many splendid plans for it, the house couldn't have been better. It was two blocks from the fashionable Fairmont and Mark Hopkins hotels; a short brisk walk from the St. Francis and Sir Francis Drake hotels. Equally close were the best men's clubs: the Pacific Union, the Bohemian, the Olympic, and the Union League, to say nothing of the Press and University clubs that were also nearby. We were handy to practically everything except the Central Police Station, and you can bet I didn't complain about that.

I furnished it with nothing but the best and launched it with a magnificent masked ball. It was magnificent, and invulnerable. No one—*almost* no one, that is—ever entered without invitation and permit.

World War II was under way and there's something about war that booms the brothel business. Young officers and cost-plus war contractors graced our parlors and bedrooms day and night. Kaiser set records in shipbuilding, working in shifts around the clock. Not to be outdone in a national emergency, we followed his good example. No sacrifice was too great to make for one's country.

The Establishment ran 'round the clock. I adopted two orphaned children. I took their name and became Marcia Owen, as I didn't think Stanford would help this pair of waifs just starting out in life. My at-home name became Marcia Owen and has been that ever since. I sign checks and legal documents that way and it's been a wonderful name in those occasional moments when it might have been inconvenient to be Sally Stanford.

The Lady of the House

Meanwhile, 1144 Pine became—connoisseurs from all over the world tell me I'm right—the finest and most distinguished pleasure house in the world. Maybe the universe. We had the most desirable customers and the most desirable girls. The girls were refined, beautiful and well behaved, and they created a stir wherever we went. I had driven a bevy of them down to the beach one day to inspect some property I own.

While in that neighborhood a charming middle-aged matron tenaciously forced her acquaintanceship upon us. She was a schoolteacher visiting relatives. She approached me as I was leaving and said, "My goodness, I have never seen such lovely and charming girls in my whole life. You must be running a famous finishing school for such delightful debutantes."

"Oh, yes, something like that," I murmured, as I moved toward the car and the girls.

She followed, saying she hoped she could ride to town with us. She was very large and the car was already crowded with my dainty debutantes.

"Oh, it will be just lovely," she insisted. "I'll just squeeze in here in the back and these two lovelies can sit on my lap."

During the short ride it developed that she was so impressed she wanted to teach at my school, saying she specialized in French literature, proper English, and of course etiquette. I explained there was no vacancy on our staff at the moment, but I would certainly keep her in mind. We dropped her off and she pressed a bit of paper into my hand with her name and address neatly written in her prim schoolteacher's handwriting.

"Do keep me in mind," she implored. "I'm so impressed."

You should have heard the girls laughing and screaming all the way back to Pine Street. Debutantes, yes. Finishing school? Maybe.

Every merchant knows the value of proper display. It was good business to arrive with a group of my beautiful girls in places people would least expect to see a madam and her stable. Many of my best customers were members of one of the most wealthy churches. It was the tradition in this church during the Christmas season to give a magnificently staged pageant of scenes pertinent to the Christmas story. It was spectacularly and beautifully done.

Knowing a flock of social lechers attended this theatrical extravaganza, I took a whole row of seats center front, and the girls and I arrived dressed to compete with the opening show of a high-fashion dress designer's collection. The scenes unfolded depicting the events leading up to the birth of Christ, and at intermission time as we strolled in the foyer smiling and nodding and being introduced to new gentlemen with non-Christmas ideas in their minds except for an extracurricular present for themselves, one of the most angel-faced debutantes suddenly got the message involving the circumstances of the Virgin Mary's pregnancy. I made no pretense to understanding the Holy Trinity, the virgin birth, or the Immaculate Conception, but I could understand a young girl's interest in details concerning her profession.

The whole message of the glorious pageant escaped her. She was interested in the practical aspect of the scene, and with the enthusiasm of sudden discovery that lights up the face of all youth, she blurted out, "You mean God sent that angel down to get the Virgin pregnant?"

"That's the story, my dear," I replied.

"You mean just like a pimp," she said, in a theatrical whisper that I was sure could be heard all over the auditorium. And before I could quiet them, another of the girls answered her with, "Well, all of the churches have been taking their cut out of that piece ever since."

I got them quieted and back to their seats and immediately

passed a new house rule. No discussions about religion. Contro-
versial subjects are just not safe.

Many of the girls went straight from Sally's to suburban
homes and did damn well at it. Just a few nights ago at my
restaurant, one of my ex-girls dropped by with her handsome
husband. Now married ten happy years, mother of six children
and a local big wheel with the PTA, she's doing o.k.

Another invested some of her money in a college degree and
today is a highly respected marriage counselor; and a couple are
social bigwigs right here in Marin County next door to Valhalla.

Of course, some of them took another route. I suspect that
Vassar, too, turned out some duds. Most of the failures tumbled
into these jackpots because some miserable pimp turned them
out on dope or involved them in crime.

On the happier side of the picture is a girl whose success story
hasn't made the *Ladies' Home Journal*, but a helluva success
story it is just the same.

If a pretty girl is like a melody, then Frankie Miller was a
whole cotton-pickin' symphony. Motion picture stars who used
to come to my place, band leaders, socialite tycoons, spoiled
playboys, all said she was the most beautiful woman they'd ever
seen. Frankie was a charmer in every way. She was the most
complete courtesan that ever graced a mattress. Incredibly
enough, she got along beautifully with the other girls. She was
so impressive as an attractive, compelling personality that some
properly connected guest suggested starting her on a career in
the entertainment world.

"Not for me, Sally," she replied. "I've crossed my bridge. I'm
on this side. I don't know what I might have been if I hadn't
turned out. I do know I'd rather be an honest prostitute than a
cheating wife or a part-time chippy. Let's forget it."

The Lady of the House

One night a client recommended by a leading member of the Pacific Union Club, the town's toniest men's club, engineered his way, with difficulty, up the stairs into our drawing room. He was a famous engineer and his recommendations were Grade A. He was conducted past the bar and finally settled in an easy chair from which he could watch the festivities and regain his strength until he was well enough to play. As his strength returned, he said to the manager in charge, who had tried to interest him in one of my girls who was very good at handling drunks: "Inebriated as I am, I'm thoroughly càpable of scratching my own ass, fighting my own battles, and selecting my own women. I desire that girl."

And he pointed to Frankie.

Frankie and her admirer were not seen for the rest of the evening. The engineer paid a tab that must have surely added a couple of zeros to someone's bill for a bridge. The next evening he engineered his sober way to Frankie and the two did a repeat. I was considering adding a surcharge for taking my star artist out of circulation. This went on for four nights. Then, he asked to see me. I told him Frankie hadn't put in an appearance yet.

"I know," he said. "She's packing her clothes. We got married this afternoon."

After I put my head together again and sorted out my whirling reaction, I listened to the rest of his story. This man's wife had been dead for over a year, leaving him with a four-year-old boy to care for. He was not only lonely, but he wanted a mother for his son.

"I've been looking the world over for her," he told me. "And here I have to find her in a whorehouse in San Francisco. But find her I did, and I'm eternally grateful. We want your blessing."

"Well, I'll be goddamned," I said, still a little dazed by this daffy marriage, one, I was sure, that had not been made in

The Lady of the House

Heaven. "Didn't Frankie have anything to say about bridges and not wanting to . . ."

"Yeah," he said. "She did give me some kind of chatter about having crossed her bridge; bridges are my specialty and I told her none I ever heard of were strictly one-way. Now, about your blessing . . ."

Well, I gave them the blessing, a champagne party on the house, no guests for that evening, and a pair of end tables for the home he was planning for her. Some Bible-hanging moralists I know would only be pleased if I finished this story with Frankie creeping back a year later with a sad tale of how it hadn't worked and begging for re-employment; but last year when I went east I was a guest of Frankie and her semi-famous husband. She thinks he's great. He still thinks she's the loveliest woman that ever came down the pike. Now, after fourteen years of domesticity and a few more children (why say how many and start every engineer's neighbor between Florida and Maine thinking?), I agree with him. I never was one to get maudlin about female beauty.

Sometimes you have to break the rules. Usually I did not encourage or allow women guests or visitors to my establishment. However, public relations and a request from the press can change a girl's mind.

One of my many newspaper pals, Bob Patterson, called and was entertaining some still-famous motion picture friends of his. The party included some of the most publicized actresses in the world. It seems to me that basically a woman who sells her emotions in bed, often pretending love and affection, is as great an actress as one who sells her beauty and emotions to the camera or the public. Personally, I trust most prostitutes further than the actresses I've known. An actress without a director can be as awkward as an undisciplined puppy off the leash. And a couple of Hollywood's female hoydens convinced me that many ac-

The Lady of the House

tresses need a tough-willed director and a leash forged from
steel. Still, I broke my rule for the press.

It was a big, fat mistake. One international beauty, more famous for her face and figure than her histrionics, barely got
through the introductions before she made like a puppy at a
party. She sat in all the men's laps, told jokes that would have
shaken the stags at an American Legion smoker, and we finally
had a helluva time subduing her from knocking on the doors of
the occupied rooms with cries of "Fire! All out!"—this being
her idea of very funny stuff.

The other, famed internationally on stage and screen as one of
the world's great, drank a half bottle of Kentucky bourbon,
chased it with Southern Comfort, let out a basso profundo laugh
and proceeded to make like a giddy child on Christmas morning.
Only her packages were closed not with pretty ribbons and
Christmas stickers, but with the zippers on my guests' pants.
Exclaiming in excited glee over the contents of each new pack-
age, she stirred up quite a caper. Needless to say, the men were
excited. But some actresses thrive on being different. When it
looked as though most of my guests were going to chase her
upstairs, she switched the scene, laughed roguishly, chased two
of my girls upstairs, locked the door from the inside and passed
out. After this caper I put the "No Ladies" rule back in full
force.

But show-business people we saw plenty.

Mark Hellinger, the director and producer, who never quite
gave up being a newspaperman, came, drank, chatted, and left as
pleasantly and as courteously as if he were being entertained in a
Pacific Heights mansion. He always left a large-sized bill for
each girl, none of whom he sampled. A singer-actor, with a far
more spectacular name, never entered the house. He ordered
two girls sent to his room at the Fairmont Hotel, gave them an
insultingly bad time, as entertainment for his audience of pals,

and then stiffed them (refused to pay). A charming fellow, he. I trust his ice water boils when he finally gets to Hell.

On the other hand, an especially sweet guy was Errol Flynn. He arrived at 1144 Pine late in the night as a sort of fugitive. It was toward the end of the war and he had wandered into Finocchio's, a bistro famous for its entertainment, advertised as presenting the world's most fabulous female impersonators. While there, a Marine had asked for Flynn's autograph in an insolent way. When he declined, the serviceman responded with a term that specified oral copulation as a Flynn weakness and preceded the phrase with the word "yellow." There was a scuffle. Flynn flattened the yokel and departed.

Scuttling a United States Marine in wartime was a little less serious than delivering an American battleship to the Japanese with Mrs. Roosevelt tied up in the captain's cabin. The wire services and newspaper headlines broke out in a hue and cry.

Flynn arrived in a taxi with his coat collar pulled up to his eyes and his hat lowered over them. I'd known him over the years and recall many pleasant visits with him. He had tried to get into his hotel, but his room was barricaded with reporters and photographers. When he called his studio the next morning, he was told to lay low. He stayed at 1144 Pine for two weeks.

We talked a lot during his stay, and for all of his humor and easy gaiety, he was most obviously an unhappy man. He was full of the many things he didn't want to do. He didn't want to work in pictures. He didn't want to grow old. And he did not want to remain married to any one woman.

"A terrible thing about getting married, Sally," he said, "is the children. Children are wonderful. They can't stay that way. They grow up to be people. And that is usually a tragedy when you think about the kind of people most people are. Right?"

But for all of his melancholy, screwy beliefs, he was an attractive, uninhibited male with a helluva lot more courage than he was given credit for. He was extremely active in the realm of amorous endeavor. Most probably he was the only customer I ever had who tested all of the talent, including both shifts, twice. He went through the place like a dose of salts.

Another well liked and extremely charming guest was Jean Sablon, the handsome, erudite singer of French songs, many of them about the Parisian street girls. *"Femmes de pavé"* he called them. As "Meester Smeeth" he had all my girls wild about him, but none did he take to the hay. A few drinks, a little conversation, an expression of thanks for a chance to get away from the conventional parties that had been stacked up for him, and Meester Smeeth was on his way.

A ham with a different flavor was Humphrey Bogart who dropped by on many of his visits to San Francisco, usually to no one's rapture or delight. The common concept of Bogie as a tough and rugged good guy, with plenty of class, proves again my point. Some actors need directors when they're let off the studio leash. We found him to be a foul-mouthed, pugnacious drunk who came around to badger, belittle, and insult the girls. When I put it to him that he was strictly not for people, he was always surprised.

"Doesn't everyone come on like this in a whorehouse," he said, "so long as they can pay big and tip larger?"

He never really got the idea. We finally had to "eighty-six" him. No class.

One famous actor flew in from his palatial home in Bel Air, spent a few weeks playing and drinking and living it up with us. One evening he gave everybody in the house $300, chartered a plane, and took us all as his guests to Reno. He offered to pay house expenses while we were away. We had a ball, though some of the girls lost their take backing his bets at the tables. So we flew back in his plane. These memories rush to my mind when his old movies are shown on television.

The Lady of the House

There are a lot more whose names and characteristics would titillate the curious and the name-droppers, but why stir that pot?

Husband Lou and I had built a charming summer place at Lake Tahoe, just a few feet down the street from the famous casinos. It's still there, long since converted to a shop. We used to go there in the summer and relax and play house in the magnificent scenery. And memories of Tahoe in the early days came back to me when I was there last summer with Arthur Godfrey when he did his show at Harrah's Club.

Tahoe is full of characters, too. One darling little old lady created quite a stir, asserting her sense of proper justice. Before the casinos came, she owned much of the lakeside property on which she grazed cattle. Casino workers and tourists cluttered up her land with debris, beer cans and trash. And when her complaints went unheeded, she met the Greyhound Buses that brought the slot-machine addicts to the clubs in droves. Dressed in a sunbonnet and cotton pinafore, she jumped aboard the newly arrived bus with two huge garbage pails filled to the brim. Before the astonished driver or amazed tourists could depart, she had strewn the contents of her buckets down the center aisle of the bus, muttering, "What you're doing to my property, I'll do back to yours."

Justice I like.

Eight

THE Establishment, 1144, was an education in itself, and if it didn't happen there, it probably hasn't happened. One motion picture star whose male beauty and appeal put his salary among the highest in the world was a lesson in himself. His several marriages produced headlines, settlements, and divorces. No heirs. Women all over the world begged for his favors, kept the postmen weary dumping their letters by the truckload at his door. And he had a specialty. Self-devotion can go too far. Jayne Mansfield, Jane Russell and Mae West are to feminine bounty what Narcissus is to the male. Alas, he could not or would not share. Exhibit his wares he did with great enthusiasm, but his was strictly a self-made treasure. I leave it to you; he disgusted my staff and that took some doing. Clinicians and psychologists have names for such contortions. He must have practiced long hours and human dignity allows me to say only that in his solo act of love, he talked constantly and we called the episode "Look Ma, no hands."

He was billed as the screen's most torrid lover.

The Lady of the House

I mentioned earlier that the waiting list of hopeful employees was bountiful. Three charming twists, Navy wives from San Diego, had a working agreement to spend their weekends profitably with us. One of my preferred guests was a well-publicized naval admiral.

You've guessed it.

They met one fateful weekend and it was quite a scene. For here he was, faced with three of his best officers' most social Navy wives. These babes really loved their extracurricular hobby.

In true admiral fashion, he sized up the situation, laughed heartily and said, "Well, ladies, we're all in this together. We know what we're here for, so what the hell, bring on the champagne and let's go to bed." The Admiral took them all to bed, a night on the town with dinner at Ernie's, back to bed again and home to San Diego. I've always liked the Navy.

And looks aren't everything, let me tell you. One eager applican was one of, if not *the,* ugliest woman in the world. Sometimes I'm amazed at the minute consistency of nature. Most people have something beautiful or handsome or spectacular about them. An otherwise plain face is often framed in magnificent hair. Some people have lovely eyes or Grecian sculptured hands. This creature was fashioned with such utmost consistency that every part of her competed with the rest in homeliness. But her earnestness and determination to work even for free moved me, and so I called in the staff to decide what we could do with her. Someone suggested a sequin veil, and we would bill her as a Harem dancer from Egypt. That might work if we kept the lights low and the guests high.

As was my custom always with new employees, I asked her to strip, for if nothing else, every girl must be, and always was, immaculate. Well, honest Injun, cross-my-heart-and-hope-to-die, I'm telling you, the rest of her was equally consistent with her face. I hope never again to view such a completely coordinated symphony of competing ugliness. Even her unmentionables had their own magnificent ugliness. Her central heating plant was strictly for go, not for show.

Beauty is only skin deep, they say, and this creature had a fervent yearning to share, so we tried. And in less time than it takes to tell this story, she was the toast of the house. This babe was so devoted to her work, so cooperative and so violent in the ecstasy she produced in my guests, she got all the business, and the other girls complained until I suggested that she set herself up and keep the profits. Like I said, you can't tell by the wrapping. I've known some beauties that were some duds.

A fortress can have disadvantages; a well-trained staff may obey orders too meticulously. You may remember the iron gate on the street and the vestibule between it and the heavy locked door.

One rule strictly enforced was that these two doors were never unlocked simultaneously. Once we had had a busy, tiring night and everyone deserved some rest. It was early in the morning and I gave orders that under no circumstances was the door to be opened or the telephone answered, and thus I learned how efficient my own staff was.

I had just gotten into my chiffon nightie, put up my hair in curlers, when the buzzer sounded. Well, I thought, I'll check it out myself. One of my admirers had sent by special delivery a huge rococo, framed, invaluable oil painting. I went down to receive it. Just as the delivery boy had put it through the iron bars of the front gate and departed, a sudden draft of wind slammed and locked the second door behind me. Trapped in my own vestibule! I beat on the door, sat on the buzzer, screamed and kicked, but to no avail; and there I was on Pine Street with the morning commuters and office workers sailing past my door, curiously looking at me in nightie, ducking not too gracefully behind an oversized painting of a voluptuous nude.

I stopped one pleasant-looking young man and asked him to phone the house number and tell them to open up and let me in. I heard the phone ringing itself off the wall, but true to the boss no one answered it. This went on for several hours, and the postman came and I asked him to telephone; and he called; again the phone rang and no answer. I was getting rather bored, annoyed and furious with the whole routine and sure as hell must have looked pretty silly ducking behind a painting trying to cover my all from the eyes of the world, being veiled only by a thin but very pretty nightdress. Finally one of the girls decided to leave, and when she opened the inner door to let herself out, I stamped upstairs disgruntled and furious. The phone rang wildly. I answered it and a pleasant male voice said, "Lady, will you please open your inner door, there's some broad in your vestibule who can't get in."

Occasionally, we got a call from someone we didn't know. Usually they mentioned the name of a well-known guest. But we had a way of further screening our callers, for I was determined to outwit the police. When such calls came, the caller would be directed to the lobby of one of the best hotels. Among our trusted employees were many taxi drivers, and the love-hopeful stranger would be given a false name. When this name was paged in the lobby of the hotel, he would find a cab waiting to bring him by a circuitous route to his pleasure. When the cabdriver was convinced that he was all right, he brought him to the establishment. A city manager of one of California's most famous cities arrived by this route. When asked his pleasure, he said, "Oh, Miss Stanford, may I please go back to the hotel lobby? That cloak-and-dagger ride was the most exciting ride that ever happened to me. I want to do it all over again!" And the son of a bitch did.

The Lady of the House

One day I was sitting at my dressing table in my apartment on Bush Street, fixing my hair and face, when out of nowhere a wild-eyed young man with a gun appeared behind me. I could see him clearly in the mirror and was a little shook when he said, "Give me all your money and your jewels, or I'll shoot."

You should know me well enough by now to lay big odds on my hanging on to what's mine. This youngster, merely passed his boyhood, seemed so nervous and desperate that I was truly frightened.

"How much do you need?" I asked.

"All you've got, and your jewels, too."

"You know this is a terrible thing to do. It won't solve anything."

"Don't talk like that," he said. "Just give me the dough."

"Well, I don't have any money here," I replied.

"Look, Sally Stanford, the two richest women in town are you and Mrs. Spreckels. I almost decided on her."

I continued putting on my makeup, taking a lot of time with my mascara, fussing with each eyelash. The young man seemed fascinated.

"Well, I'm honored at your decision," I told him. "Why do you need the money?"

"Lady, I don't want talk. I just want the dough."

"Young man, you'd better give me that gun. If it should go off, you'll have a terrible problem."

"Give me the dough," was his reply to me.

His hands were shaking and his eyes were wild, but I persisted.

"Tell me, sonny, where is your mother?"

"She's not here; and don't talk like that."

"You must have a terrible problem to drive you to do this awful thing."

At this he started to look around the room and shake.

"Give me the gun. It might go off."

He handed me the gun and burst into tears. We talked for a while and I gave him fifty dollars and my phone number and told him to call me. The next day he called and thanked me for saving him from a terrible crime. That was an easy one. The next time the burglars were tougher; there were more of them, and they were more determined.

Came the day when I looked murder straight in the face, and the only reason this book has been written in the first person singular today is because on the 5th of February, 1947, I had a strong objection to being killed, and I refused to cooperate with the killers.

It was a cold, foggy morning, a day that is made for murder. It was the kind of morning when you open your eyes, take a fast look at the gray mist pressing gloomily against the window-pane, then quickly plunge your head into the pillow for more sleep.

I had worked late the night before and it was almost dawn before I pulled my big car into the driveway of my home at 1977 Clay Street. My premonition mechanism was working overtime and I felt a strange uneasiness about leaving the car and entering the house. A young man from next door whom I had seen in the area before was leaving for work and I asked him to walk me to the front of the house.

Once inside, I went apprehensively from room to room, checking for signs of something suspicious. It wasn't like me to feel nervous about anything, but *this* morning I felt something was wrong. Instead of sleeping in my own bedroom, I slept in another one in the other part of the house. I spent some time changing the normal hiding places for my jewels and money and slipped my keys into the pillowcase under my head, instead of just under the pillow. Right or wrong, I wasn't going to take a chance on my premonition being correct, as it usually was, and my being unprepared.

Finally, I fell into a restless sleep, not knowing the events that were building up to one of the most frightening experiences of my life.

The day before, two desperate and experienced thugs had cased my home in expectations of robbing it, and me. They had found a note in one of the milk bottles outside the door telling the milkman to ask my maid, Elsie Hill, for the check that was due him.

At about 9:15 A.M., Elsie opened the kitchen door a crack and saw a young man in a white uniform, milk bottles in his hand, a smile on his face. Thinking it was the milkman, she went to get the check I had made out for him. As she opened the door a little wider to give it to him, he pushed it open and entered the room, a .45 automatic in his hand. From around the corner of the door came his accomplice, carrying a .38 Smith & Wesson revolver.

They were also carrying a full head of narcotic steam, having loaded up with "H" before coming to call. Their names were Mark Monroe and Thomas Sitler, and they were veterans—experts at mayhem and mutilation, graduates of San Quentin and other institutions of applied violence.

They grabbed Elsie by the hair, swung her to the floor and while one of them stifled her screams, the other beat her to a bloody pulp. That was so she'd get the general idea.

Their persuasive methods failed to get her to tell them where I kept my jewels and money, so they tied her up and came upstairs.

The first thing I remember was the sensation of a hand under my pillow, feeling ever so slowly around underneath my head. I opened my eyes and looked up into the cruelest face I'd ever seen. He had a mask covering half of it, but his eyes stared at me sadistically. Perhaps it was his constant staring that awakened me.

My first thought was that it was a dream, and when that passed, my mouth opened automatically and a scream came from my throat. His hand went over my face and mouth and he raised the gun and slammed it down hard on my head. He hit me four times, stunning me. I had put up my waist-long hair in two coronet braids and they helped to cushion the crushing impact of the blows. With each blow the thug hissed, "Shut up . . . SHUT UP!" through his clenched teeth.

His partner entered the room and took over where his friend left off. I began to struggle again and he slammed down on my face and head with the butt of his gun. Eight times the metal hit my flesh and the blood poured over my face and pillow. I lay dazed. During the struggle, one of their face masks came off, and while he struggled to get it back on, his partner held my head in his hand, saying, "Don't look at him. If you want to live, don't look at him." But he was too late, and I had gotten a vivid picture in my mind of the face of Mark Monroe.

They placed the muzzles of their revolvers at my temples and tried to get me to tell them where the jewels and money were hidden. Remembering how a friend had once told me about the value of "surprise" moves when in danger, I instinctively grabbed for the guns and thrust them up and away from my face. With speed given me by fear of losing my life, I leaped from the bed to the window, opening it a few inches and screaming at the top of my lungs.

Across the street two painters were working. They looked up and caught a glimpse of me at the window. It flashed in my mind to jump from the window, hoping I'd hit the heavy bushes below and miss the cement. Before I could take another step, Monroe and Sitler were upon me again. They threw me to the floor, kicking me and cursing. One of them looked out of the window and saw the commotion below. He announced to his partner that this party was no longer a private affair.

At that point I was about to lose consciousness. I felt as though I were drowning. The two men clattered down the stairs like a pair of berserk animals. I stumbled to the door and down the stairs, almost falling head over heels.

Outside, one of the painters had taken the number "57" from the back of the rented car the two men drove. They had rented it from Aero-U-Drive, and Mark Monroe had used his driver's license to get the car.

Next door, Mrs. Patty La Mogge crawled down the corridor of her home, her broken leg and cast dragging behind her, to her telephone to call the police. She had heard my screams and was determined to help.

When I got downstairs and released Elsie from her bonds, she wanted to call the police herself. I said No! No one knew where I was living. I felt it was best for my son if they didn't know my past life or who I really was.

I sat at the dining room table, my head down on my arms. The blood from my head seeped onto the table and moved toward the edge, threatening to fall onto my beautiful carpet. I remember telling Elsie to clean it up quick. A few seconds passed and then a knock on the door came to my ears. My next-door neighbor had succeeded and the police had arrived. Elsie let them in.

The police apprehended the hoodlums in short order. I was in the hospital now and was there for a long time. At the trial both men denied any knowledge of the attack and were shocked and distressed at my identification of them.

Sitler's defense depended upon his confederate Monroe, and this slick character produced a dame named Barbara Keilhammer who blithely attested that all of the previous night, and far into the morning of the assault, Monroe was happily in bed with her. She added a few clinical details concerning their lengthy cohabitation and threw in some compliments for her man's virility.

The police, however, turned up information proving that were she speaking the truth about Monroe's sexual powers, it must have been the long-distance record of sexual intercourse. Miss Keilhammer was unquestionably in Chicago at the time. The poor dame won herself a perjury conviction for her loyalty; Monroe and Sitler drew a hung jury, and while out on bail, jumped to Mexico and were finally brought back by Red Maloney, the bondsman. They were sent to Folsom for long terms of imprisonment.

Sometime later I made a trip to Los Angeles to fight the State's decision to gas another woman, a woman called Barbara Graham. This poor, broken-down, hustling broad and Tenderloin tramp was made to order for the role society decided she should play. She was bad. The documented floozy! And after it was over, Metro-Goldwyn-Mayer, with Susan Hayward starring in the role, turned out a profitable movie based on her story.

It was obvious that she had been a psychiatric problem, emotionally sick for years.

I worked very hard to save her life. When I went to picket outside the penitentiary on the day she died, reporters asked me why I was there. I ask you, what would you say at a time like that? I didn't offer the information that she had never worked for me; nor that the last time I had seen Barbara Graham was shortly after she'd testified, as Barbara Keilhammer, to a phony alibi for a man who tried to kill me. She told me she was sorry for her lie; she asked me to understand the why of it. I understood.

So they killed her. It wasn't without a fight, however, upon the part of many of us. And at one point I was promised by Governor Goodwin Knight that she'd be given a break. Something happened to that promise, or maybe Goodie defines a break differently than I.

Barbara wasn't a good girl. She wasn't even a good bad girl. Yet moving her into Tamalpais Cemetery, outside of San Rafael, solved nothing.

Caryl Chessman's case became practically a full-time job with me. I talked with almost every one of the many persons associated with his defense. Some were hungry and energetic vultures. Others were dedicated to saving his life. It became crystal clear that in the final analysis the determination of one man, Miller Leavy, Deputy District Attorney of Los Angeles, was stronger than the combined good intentions of all the thousands throughout the world who tried to save him.

I was in the parking area in front of San Quentin with many others who felt as I did when this unfortunate man was poisoned by the State of California. I had been waiting there for a number of hours. When the final word came, the tears naturally came to my eyes.

A reporter for a San Francisco newspaper was standing nearby. That evening I read that "Sally Stanford cried when Chessman's death was announced."

I felt that this occurrence was not worth reporting. It *does* seem a matter of forethought and consideration that a woman's tears over the misery and murder of a human being is considered news.

Is there any other reaction?

Nine

WITH the cream of society (male half) calling on me, **I** began to regard myself as an unpublished member of the Blue Book set. It was then I was publicly labeled a society woman in the newspaper columns of the San Jose *Mercury*. My social success lasted through one whole edition of the paper. It all happened as a result of my marriage to Bob Gump. And the young reporter who covered the deal wrote: "The socially prominent Sally Stanford married Robert Livingston Gump."

The item was picked up in the city by the smart-talking columnists and much was made of the hassle caused by the managing editor of the suburban paper. This gentleman, whose columns were liberally sprinkled with the dropped names of the Peninsula's reigning socialites, raised hell with the youngster and demanded how he'd gotten the idea that Sally Stanford was a socialite.

"She had a mink coat," he replied with shattering simplicity. Maybe that's how you find them down the Peninsula.

Maybe we weren't as precious as the members of the Burlingame Country Club, but we were exclusive and allowed some of its best members to join our elite lechers, and this included a few that were as daffy as they were pedigreed. They had that over-hormoned, aging millionaire from the Monterey Peninsula. He impressed himself and my girls with his virility by making like a Bernard McFadden advertisement. He would bulge his muscles and tear telephone books in half. One night he tore up every damn book in the house, and sent over to his club for more. For weeks the only numbers we could find were those left in the column closest to the binding.

Another banking tycoon was notorious for "civic betterment." The newspapers loved to talk about his uplifting programs. His enjoyment was to lie prone and nude while the lady of his pleasure walked on him barefooted.

One night his mount was a twist named Elise, whom I'd been trying to persuade to take off a few pounds. Somehow she managed, during a stroll, to disengage her client's sacroiliac. The poor man nearly went out of his mind with pain. It took quite a posse of us to calm him down and soothe him into his clothes and out into the night. A day or so later, I read in Herb Caen's column that a recent guest had checked into the St. Francis Hospital for treatment. It seems he had suffered a back injury in a "traffic accident"—which was quite true when you pause to think of it.

Never, however, did we encounter the kind of a health problem that gave poor Mabel Malotte such a bad time with one of her customers. A wealthy Chinese gentleman, one of the most prominent patriarchs of Chinatown, was in the saddle and trying hard for a record score when he suddenly joined his ancestors. It wasn't a development that immediately came to the attention of one and all because the young lady who was in charge of his happiness assumed for a moment or two that he had merely fallen asleep.

When the truth became known, Mabel was sincerely distressed; she had not only lost an old and valued customer, but she had a corpse to dispose of. No right-thinking madam would consider having recourse to the conventional facilities under such circumstances. It would bring not only notoriety to the newly departed, but a helluva lot of official questions. Mabel and the young lady in whose arms the gentleman had gone to his reward hoisted him between them, one of his arms over each of their shoulders, and watching for the moment when Bay Street was completely empty, they took the old gentleman for his last midnight stroll.

This may be the first revelation for the Pow Yick Goy Tong which laid his corpse to rest in great ceremony a few days later. No one could explain the circumstances of his discovery, for as the misty blue dawn lighted a Bay Street doorway, he was seated there with his clothes piled neatly at his side. Mabel mailed his wallet to the tong, the money intact. She didn't even subtract the usual tariff. She figured this last one was on the House.

We had our moments, too, at Chez Stanford, and our kooks as well.

One of the problems of a well-publicized and fascinating business is that the word gets around. Everyone knows more about it than you do, and at the same time the most important self-protective device is to conduct a palace of pleasure in the manner that everything can be rumored and nothing can be proved.

It was my purpose to be known and patronized, simultaneously not to be caught or victimized, and this schizoid route to adventure brought about the most prolonged, ardent and devoted suitor in my life. This was a romance of many years. Devotion with some lovers is a full-time job. This Romeo I admired. He was determined to make me his. He devoted his professional lifetime to the pursuit of Sally.

It is a moot question whether I played Juliet to his Romeo or a sort of Moby Dick to his Captain Ahab. He never put his harpoon into me. Sergeant John Dyer was the Don Quixote of law enforcement. He had dedicated himself to a crusade. He was going to "get" Sally Stanford.

He often worked at it on his own time, unpaid. He spent his own money on it. There's no explaining love. John spent his entire police lifetime, and like the sportsman he was, determined to bag the largest fish, he angled for me. I had known John since my freshman days in the Tenderloin, and Dear John was many things—honest, clean, well-shaven, good at matching coins, kind to his wife and mother, and determined.

Two gentlemen showed up one afternoon, a Mr. Grossman and a Mr. Smith. They wanted girls. My premonition gong began to chime, so I had Wong Hee usher them into a room equipped with two-way communication. In short, it was bugged.

I talked with them briefly and amiably and asked for their identification. Now the gong was bonging like Big Ben. Mr. Grossman was a drapery goods salesman and had a large sample case of handsome fabrics. He presented Mr. Smith as an old friend of his from out of town, and he just couldn't let good old Smitty leave town without visiting Sally's, could he? Ha, ha, ha. That was before I left the room.

Wong Hee served them with a drink, and, as instructed, refused to take their money. Grossman tried to tuck a few bills in Wong's pocket.

When I picked up the intercom listener in the next room, it turned out Grossman was pretty pleased with himself:

"She's in the bag," he said.

Smith was a little less sure. "I don't know. I think she's giving us the oakie-doak."

Grossman again made with the big ha, ha, ha, an obnoxious variety of bray. "Don't you believe it! It was these drapery samples that did it. She figures on conning me out of some free material. Women forget everything else when there's a chance of getting something for free. We're in solid; Johnnie will love it."

Not much doubt Johnnie will love it, I told myself, as I headed for a window from which I could survey the neighborhood. Sure enough, a police car was parked at the end of the street and another in the next block. Peering from a doorway of an apartment building across the way and as conspicuous as a zebra at a christening was my old sweetheart from San Francisco's finest, Sergeant John Dyer. He had the same expression on his face that Tiny Tim had when he saw the Christmas goose. He expected great things from playboys Grossman and Smith.

Wong Hee whispered in my ear. "Mr. Glossman, he poleeseman," he said. "I see him all the time on Turk Street. One time I see him allest lady; big sheet heel, Mr. Glossman, but I think have othah name."

"I think so, too, Wong, but give him another drink, smile like you love him forever, don't take a dime, and I'll get the girls on their way."

And I did.

I knew they'd be pinched as soon as they reached the pavements, but that was all right. On the sidewalk they were just wholesome citizens, loaded with Constitutional rights, and Johnnie and his nightstick grenadiers could arrest until they ran out of handcuffs.

I returned to the frolicsome couple and broke the news to them that all of the secretaries were gone for the day.

"Secretaries!" said Grossman.

"Yes, you wanted to give some dictation, didn't you, my dear? We've got the best secretarial service in town."

"Frigged, after all this trouble," said Smitty sourly. "I told you so, you smart bastard!"

The Lady of the House

Grossman was winking at me, his eyelids working overtime, trying to get the trolley back on the track.

"Girls! That's what we want! You know what we want, Sally. Dames! For *this* kind of secretarial work."

And he made a gesture with his hand that has always made me a little ill, even after a quarter century in the business. It was no effort at all for me to look offended and shocked.

"I certainly don't know what you want. Just look out of the window and you'll see the young ladies leaving for their homes, although I can't understand why all those men are accosting them. . . ."

A short gander out the window convinced Grossman of his exit cue. His mutterings did not sound well from the lips of a self-respecting drapery salesman. Gathering up his samples, Mr. Smith followed him gloomily to the street.

I was at the Hall of Justice with a bondsman almost before the girls arrived with John's escort service, and before the ink was dry on the blotter, the dismissals were arranged; the girls had been booked as vagrants, a face-saving gesture for the police. I was a little sorry for John. To cast and rehearse a well-planned scene is at best a gamble; to close on opening matinee frustrates the best of us.

As I left the Hall on the way out of the bail bond office, I passed Dyer's police car parked in front. A swatch of drapery material had been carelessly tossed in the back. I paused and jotted a love note on the back of the bail receipt, and carefully pinned it to the most scarlet brocaded sample from Mr. Grossman's kit:

DEAR JOHN,
    Your draperies are showing.

Love,
SALLY

The Lady of the House

One Sunday afternoon a few weeks later, business was more social than sexual, and Jackson, my aide-de-camp, approached me with the odd little secret smile he wore when something particularly unusual had happened, or was about to happen.

"Santa Claus," he said, "may be a little early this year." He handed me my binoculars. "There certainly is something worth looking for on the chimney of the house next door."

I had myself a look. A man was climbing about on the next-door roof. I recognized him and I was touched. It was, of course, John. There he was, always thinking of me, working on his day off, in his best suit. It made me feel sort of special. Jackson and I watched him for quite a while. And I caught my breath when his foot slipped as he tested storm drains obviously too weak to carry his weight, and I prayed for him as he made the jump over the narrow chasm between that building and mine. When he hit my roof, I phoned the Central Station and reported a prowler.

Months ahead I had installed a barbed-wire jungle over my roof. A girl can't be too careful. John was fully equipped, and his wire cutters were making a narrow path when the San Francisco prowl car service arrived. From the street two harness bulls, with revolvers drawn, ordered the poor man to descend to the street. Sheepishly, they put their guns away when they recognized the "prowler." I joined the officers in the street. Dusk had settled on the scene, and I could hardly be blamed for failing to recognize an old friend with the goddamnedest expression on his face.

"Take him away," I said. "I won't prefer charges. This poor lad obviously has his problems and couldn't be responsible for what he was doing. Take good care of him, mind you!"

Our romance took on the proportions of a contest, and my phone brought many declarations of John's attention to me. I learned to recognize Dear John's voice with its South of Market burr. John was a man of one purpose and one voice. His imitations and impersonations fooled no one. Once I picked up the telephone.

"Hello, Sally. This is Dr. Robinson. Can I come over?"

It was like Maurice Chevalier trying to imitate Sophie Tucker. I recognized John Dyer before he hit the third syllable.

"You must have the wrong number, Doctor. No one is ill here."

"Oh, you remember me, Sally. I was there with Dr. Miller. You know Dr. Miller."

There must be a Dr. Miller in everyone's life, and physicians are supposed to be welcome everywhere.

"I certainly do remember Dr. Miller. His last visit here I'll remember for a long while. He got sick all over my Persian rugs and gave me a bum check. Any friend of his is no friend of mine."

Had my mother been a spaniel, the angry word that came through the wire might have been appropriate.

"Goddamnit, Sally. I'll get the Fire Department to tear that gate down and snatch you out of there if it's the last goddamn thing I do."

"Why Dr. Robinson! I'm surprised at your professional language. Now you just behave yourself, or I'll report you to Sergeant Dyer of the Police Department and have him throw you in the 'bucket.' Meanwhile, may I suggest, Doctor, that you heal yourself? Try an aspirin, a cool shower, and a good night's sleep. Good night, Doctor."

And I joined the ladies.

In a short time a Yellow Cab arrived at the front gate. Jackson went down to answer the bell and was jovially greeted by a large man in an obviously rented tuxedo that did not go with the clumsy shoes he was wearing. The cab, and its driver, remained at the curb. I recognized the satin-lapeled gentleman,

The Lady of the House

Marion Overstreet, a police inspector with the Vice Detail, playing courier to John's frustrated love urges.

"I'm a member of the Bohemian Club," he announced to Jackson. "I'd like to spend a little money in your joint. Open the gate, Mac."

San Francisco's Bohemian Club boasts of the most elite membership. Someone hoped that the mention of his name would be an "Open Sesame" at 1144 Pine. Incongruous dialogue and costuming loused up that act. The bulge on the hip didn't help create the proper illusion.

From my balcony seat I called down "Who's there?"

Inspector Overstreet drew himself up in his best imitation millionaire playboy style. "I'm a local clubman," he said, "and I'd like . . ."

". . . To take us all to your private club, but not tonight. Would your cabbie like to come inside, too? John, Sergeant John! Over there, behind the wheel, you look simply divine in a taxi driver's uniform. Have you decided to do some honest work for a change?"

They climbed in the cab, jammed the gears into high, and took off.

But even if John never quite made it through the front door to put the jibes on me, he did get a call through to the house and someone accepted a requisition for the services of a young lady to date "a visiting lumberman from Seattle," who was staying at the Sir Francis Drake Hotel.

Not one to turn business away, I had a girl escorted to the Drake by one of my drivers, who went up to the room with her and was startled to observe that the visiting lumberman's pants were held up with a wide leather belt, and that whatever was slung on it under the coat was most obviously not a sawmill. That did it. The two started back for the elevator. They never made it; the girl was saved the difficulty of facing a pinch involving an overt act. We were all in a better position for legal repartee.

Later, in court, when asked what she was doing knocking on the door of a strange man's room on the tenth floor of a downtown hotel, she stated she thought he was an old friend of her father's. John's boys tailed her and her escort from 1144 Pine to the hotel. This established a rather awkward link. They described as part of the evidence "a tomato-red convertible."

It was obvious they had captured a tomato, but unless her escort could be described as a convertible, I knew nothing about the matter. Furthermore, for court purposes, I didn't know that tomato from the Duchess of Windsor. That was a close call. Perhaps, had John Dyer chosen to woo the Furies as ardently as he chased me, they would not have frowned on his efforts. There was no Sally in his net.

A former client of mine used to spend many hours in the Sportsmen's Room telling how he had spent years and a fortune bringing to net the largest bass in the lake. When he caught it, he removed the lure from its mouth and turned it free. For him, the game would have ended had he not had that great bass to return to again.

Once in my house on Bush Street, John and his bully boys staged a raid. As we were herded toward the pie wagon, Sergeant John signaled me out and said, "You, stand over there. We don't want you." I know how the largest bass in the stream felt when the hook was taken out of its mouth and the cool, fresh water flowed through its gills again.

Just before the House of Stanford closed, John Dyer asked for retirement from the force. He said he had been afflicted with a heart attack, and after recovering, he reported to the Disability Board. Dyer told the Board that he felt he should be retired with a pension, because his heart trouble, he claimed, was brought on by years of devotion and extracurricular hours spent

The Lady of the House

trying to catch Sally. Shortly after he got his pension, he died; his everloving heart gave out from his exertions.

I, for one, was sincerely saddened. He was an old adversary, but when the game was over the excitement died. The contest we played was neither unkind nor ill-meant, and shortly after his funeral, a close friend of John's made this remark:

"You know, Sally, John spoke of you throughout that whole crazy feud as though secretly he loved you."

Maybe some people would not have liked that, nor would others have understood it, I am sure. But I did.

It was during World War II that one of John's boys, a stereotype of every Irish policeman in the world, reported this event. Up the street a few hundred yards from the establishment was a boardinghouse filled with Marines. And they were a lively bunch. Late one frolicsome night a girl ran out of that house and was caught, completely nude, a few yards from my front door. When she was apprehended, her description of where she came from pointed the finger at Sally's house. My inventive Jackson answered the policeman's ring. The Irish policeman said he must come in and find out what funny things went on in this house. Jackson, never at a loss, said "This is an exclusive ballet school, and you cannot come in without a warrant."

In less time than it takes to tell it, the Fire Department arrived, threatening to knock the doors down with axes, claiming a fire had been reported. There was nothing to do but let them and John in, and there were my prettiest girls, doing their arabesques and pliés, positions one, two, and three in the great classical manner. Oh, we had some culture at our finishing school.

--<< 147 >>--

Ten

WE were getting the real international lechers now, in the spring of '45. The United Nations delegates were very large stuff in San Francisco. Prominent society hostess types were feverish in attempts to outdo each other with the foreign sauce and spice these imports inspired. It was a romp, let me tell you!

Had Sergeant John Dyer managed a raid during their stay with me, I'd have claimed diplomatic immunity and grabbed him as a hostage or prisoner-of-war or something. Foreign diplomats availed themselves plenty of everything the house had to offer, including mattress sport. Some of them spent more time dipping the wick in the feathers than they did at the United Nations deal. Several never left my place!

Since these boys were very large and juicy items with the State Department, we worked overtime to keep the foreign relations department in sweet rapport.

Other than taste the hors d'oeuvres and test the talent, these lads spent more time arguing and quarreling among themselves than you'd believe possible. I was amazed. I was certainly amazed. After seeing them work out on each other and tabulating the reports of their flounders *à deux, trois et quartre*, it was no mystery to me that the world's dilemmas were mostly incompleted passes. According to the reports I still read about some of these yo-yo's, they still delight in lousing things up at the United Nations.

The press reported that Sally Stanford was the unofficial hostess with the mostess for the whole shebang. There were a few incidents at the Establishment that kept us in the journals. A young reporter who wanted to get to the bottom of things, where the action was, brought several European delegates around with their wives. He failed to tell them we had a little more than a bar and a salon. Well, the stuff hit the fan when these lads met their international neighbors without wives lolling about negotiating deals other than national.

It wasn't getting caught with their diplomacies down that rocked the boat; it was the wives present that precipitated a verbal battle. All was calm later when these same eager buckos' wives were sent to garden parties down the Peninsula. The delegates returned wifeless and joined the party.

Meanwhile, Elsa Maxwell, the world's heavyweight reporter, covered the opening sessions from her pew at the Opera House, where the actual sessions took place. Elsa arranged a few international picnics and balls for the foreign set. Wives were abundant; diplomatic husband delegates were often busy at "special Plenary Sessions," "preparing a few well-chosen words" and "making contacts." Sally's parties were never short of men.

Russian, Chinese, Czech, English, Norwegian, and Mexican delegates found their way and felt very much at home. But it was the Arabians, Hindus, Egyptians and the Pakistani that were the attention grabbers. What a colorful bunch of stallions these! They really knew what they wanted. All the news journals were full of it. Dress and hat designers were inspired by the magnificent robes, the intricate turbans and the sumptuous jewels of these playboys. Everywhere they went they commanded attention and excitement. They created big excitement for me.

Except for the death of President Roosevelt, a Charlie Chaplin paternity suit, the death of Hitler and Mussolini shot, these Middle East lads crowded everything else out of the headlines. I had at that time a very handsome woman who served as a lieutenant-in-charge along with Jackson, my ever faithful. Rosanna was terribly hep. She had known some success in the theater and weathered several torrid romances with major motion picture moguls. She was magnetic, fey and very fond of the bottle. Aside from the time she arrived as a character witness for me high on the cork, she was mostly efficient and full of hell.

It was about this time one of the senior lechers of a well-graduated social family was trying to score often and noticeably as the sex athlete of the century. In the center of a social moment, this gonadal gentleman would shout out: "I want to spend the night with the most beautiful girl in the house. I want her all to myself. I'll pay Two Hundred Dollars—No, Three Hundred— She's Mine!"

This scene was taking place simultaneously with the biggest night ever of the turbaned and white-robed and bejeweled knights of the desert and the Nile, who were keeping everything very colorful all over the place. Every poon nook and cranny was occupied. I sent our ambitious social scion to the maid's room and told him as soon as the vote was taken and the most beautiful maiden was prepared for him, she would slip into the room. In the excitement and bedlam that followed, we completely forgot the amorous, darling old gent. At a later hour Rosanna, a little juiced and exhausted, went to that socialite's bed and arms. She rose earlier than he the next morning and reported a very romantic episode. Our Peninsular social lion said he, too, was delighted. Like I say, all cats look gray at night.

That was the night the sheikhs of the U.N. learned a thing or two. One of the clan had phoned early in the day saying a dozen or so of them would arrive and wanted GIRLS. Rosanna took the order and wrote it on a pad near the phone. Actually, she was never famous for the legibility of her handwriting. With a little grape ferment on her lips, she managed to create a situation that still makes me warm up with delight and amusement.

The order was for *no Jewish girls*. Rosanna had forgotten to make that small diagonal line between the top of the first vertical line of the "N" and the second vertical line. What appeared on the pad was 110 Jewish girls. I arrived late in the afternoon, picked up that pad and hit the telephone! I called everyone in town including the competition and begged, bartered, and pleaded for girls who might look a little Jewish.

A full lifetime of dealing with people from all over the world has convinced me that there is no definite national face. There are defined stereotypes yes, but even with the genius of God in arranging two eyes, one nose, and one mouth, all in multitudinous designs, who is to say that Dolores Del Rio and the Virgin Mother were not cut from the same voluptuous piece of cloth? Certainly not me!

Well, I rounded up twenty-five lovelies and figured I could run them in shifts and make it seem like one hundred and ten. I was, nonetheless, very concerned about the required Jewishness of the order. How would anyone go about proving such a thing? I tore out of the house and made for the most sumptuous Jewish temple in the Bay area. I made an appointment with the rabbi and hoped I could solve this problem.

"Rabbi, I have been concerned for a long time with joining your faith. It seems to me that all non-Jewish religions are in one way or another a revamping of the ancient truths and facts."

In a few moments I got to the vital question and discovered

that there is a religious symbol indigenous to a properly born and devout Jew—a mezuzah!

Determined to please and fill an important order, I purchased a few dozen mezuzahs. The girls were given one each and instructed to make sure that their playmates would see them before the games were over. I felt safe and pleased with myself. The afternoon and evening papers carried reports that the Jews and the Arabs had argued and quarreled at the afternoon conference —a Jewish agency for Palestine registered a complaint against the official circulation of the Pact and League of Arab States, and a third journal held that Arab and Jewish accord might be possible. I was determined to do my bit.

International relations I liked and the customer is most often right as long as he is paying. The Near Eastern group was attracting so much attention that one society editor interviewed a delegate on native customs. Believe me, she would have done better to have interviewed me. Her story went to the effect that San Francisco hostesses can learn hospitality from these venerable people. No one, she wrote, not even a stranger, is ever turned away. Well, I felt, not to be outdone, they could stay as long as their oil wells, jewels and money held out.

The tall, dark and amorous men arrived. We had them check their jeweled daggers and swords before entering the arena of games. The men arranged themselves in groups around the salon and the whole thing looked like a Cecil B. De Mille production of *Scheherezade* just before the storytelling twist took over the entertainment. My pseudo-Jewish houris, each with mezuzah, were parading and mingling with the guests.

Rosanna entered, elegant and radiant and bubbling all over the place. I took her aside: "Jesus, honey, why didn't you call me when you got that order? I've had a day finding 110 Jewish girls—"

The Lady of the House

"Jewish . . . Jewi . . . O migawd, Sally, what have you done? They'll kill them. . . . They'll wreck the place. They'll probably kill us!"

One look at Rosanna's flush of a bilious chartreuse blushing and I knew she was kidding me not. I rushed her to the kitchen and showed her the note. Rosanna picked up the pencil and drew in the missing diagonal line between the two vertical ones. One side of my head kept coming apart as I tried to put the other side together.

I called one of the girls to the kitchen. I alerted Jackson and sent Rosanna to the reception room to get the girls wise. Every goddamn houri in the scene was making a big thing of her mezuzah and the tallest, most regal chieftain of the tribe beckoned me to his side.

"Madame Stanford," said the most sinister voice I have ever heard, "what are those—those things the girls are waving at us?"

"Oh, those mez—things— Oh those things . . . those . . . yes, those are the latest and most wonderful American contraceptive!"

A curious man, he. He then asked to have a demonstration. And a demonstration he got. After those colorful romantic desert types departed, you should have heard Rosanna, Jackson and the girls roar with laughter about the mezuzahs in the kazuzahs.

The next afternoon at the Opera House the turbaned and robed, bejeweled and satisfied delegates eated a great stir. The International Press was covering the event. Harry Truman had opened the scene. The huge black automobile brought my guests to the steps of the Opera House. They, their bodyguards, and the interpreter spoke briefly into the battery of microphones. It came out like this:

"We are happy to be able to attend. We are sure some good will come of it."

The Lady of the House

Me? I still am damn careful how I cross my T's and dot my I's when I take pen in hand.

But all the customers we were getting were not right out of *Arabian Nights*. The postwar years produced a lot of pathological drinkers; many were men I'd known years before who had been acceptable and respectable. This created a problem. How do you tell an old friend and a valued customer that he has become a rum-bum and is no longer welcome? Some wives became problems too, in that they were convinced friend husband was making deposits in other accounts rather than the piggy bank at home. The Establishment at 1144 Pine Street had a most wonderful cactus garden. A former owner had traveled far and wide collecting these interesting plants. They had been arranged on a terrace by a landscape architect with great taste and charm. Except to show it off upon occasion to a horticulturist, I paid it little attention. It served a fine purpose one prickly afternoon.

A customer of many years had put suspicion in his wife's mind. She had demanded a visit to me to find out, as she put it, "What's going on . . . that's what I want to know, what's going on?" They arrived about teatime and I received them in the full elegance of the Court. After a few moments chatting with them, I saw no immediate profit in that route and I suggested that the husband take a stroll in the cactus garden while his dear wife and I had some chance to get acquainted with girl talk.

Jackson knew him well. He ushered him through the garden right into a young charmer's eager arms. The wife and I chatted away and I explained that many men came to this palace of beauty as a sort of second club. It was a place where they could meet other men in a relaxed and elegant atmosphere of refined beauty. Many a man came to get rid of bothersome troubles and to ease off the horrible tensions of the business world.

The Lady of the House

She exclaimed at the beauty of the place, she was overwhelmed at the gorgeous appointments—and the business of the rooms upstairs was not mentioned. I don't know whether she was lulled by the surroundings or by me.

In time the husband returned looking very relaxed and refined and soothed by beauty. They prepared to leave and as I was escorting them to the front door, the wife turned to her husband and sweetly murmured, "Did you enjoy the cactus garden, my dear?"

"Oh, yes, completely."

Jackson, whose timing and sense of comedy were always precious, came forth with a potted cactus and presented it to her with a courtly bow. There is, it happens, a cactus called the hairy old man. It has a facsimile resemblance to a phallus sprouting long matted gray hairs. This hairy old man was Jackson's choice as a proper parting gift for her.

For as long the husband lived, the wife called me periodically and reported the progress of her treasured cactus plant. I always had hoped for the opportunity to play marriage counselor, and I had scored with her. She was very nice.

Another wife, not so nice, raised such a hell with her husband that he arrived alone with blood running down his face and a handful of his own front teeth. Some slugger, that babe. I cleaned him up and had one of my drivers take him to my personal dentist. He did not return. Wouldn't you think she'd have gained more playing a little heavier as a courtesan and a little less a female prizefighter?

Some wives, amazingly, began to bring their husbands and ask to participate in the games. Unless I knew them very well, I refused. Today there is a plague down the Peninsula of wife swapping and cozy little arrangements right out of *The Decameron*. One muscular, narrow-hipped guy, the constant companion of a retired social couple, told me at the bar in Valhalla recently, "Secretary to her and plaything to both. Sometimes, I wake up and don't know which I've been the most of . . . husband or wife!"

"Too bad I've gone legit." I smiled at him. "You need a better broker—or at least a manager."

That unholy trinity make the papers frequently as pillars of society.

Then, as now, there were a few nauseous sicknesses of soul and psyche loose. My phone took to ringing at odd hours and the most cultured and cultivated masculine voice would say things of a completely vile and incredible nature.

When I tell you it is vile, you had better believe it. This was damned unusual. I put the telephone company's security department on these calls. They were traced to and trapped the most handsome, best-mannered, oldest, unwisest and outstanding member of the most solidly social family in San Francisco. This man is received in the best homes and his family is mentioned almost daily in the social pages. He was frightened silly by his entrapment. This, he assumed, was an impossibility. I requested that the authorities merely tell him that a repetition of his silly, sickening way of getting his jollies would result in the immediate notification of his family. That stopped it as far as my phone was concerned. But who knows what dark alley he has chosen as a proper place to sublimate his evil urges—burning churches? Peeping in sorority house bathrooms? Stealing undies from Wash-o-mats?

And if the customers were changing, so were the girls. The times were a mishmash smorgasbord. In the early days most of the women who came my way, though beautiful and unstereotyped, were professionals. They left their complications and their troubles at home. They did their work with the ease of a square peg fitting a square hole. But now, with Dr. Freud's patois commoner than cuss words, the girls arrived with exotic and neurotic ideas and plans.

Some had degrees from universities and took to writing case histories of their clients. Others would attempt mattress psychoanalysis and one wrote notes which she said were the basis of a motion picture script that would be the greatest spectacular of all. Hadn't she heard of the Hays office?

The ones who seemed happiest were the ex-wives of the country club set who set themselves up charging their ex-husbands' colleagues for the little things they had tried for free back in suburbia.

I remember many of these ladies well. Most made their decisions more deliberately, faced their chores more professionally with clearer heads than many a dame of the downtown Tenderloin. Many married well and stayed that way.

Ruth B. was a pretty little blonde with violet eyes and a flair for quoting the Bible, but correctly. She also had a deep and complete understanding of most of the salty obscenities in Italian, French, Spanish and Oriental variations. She left me to work on an assembly-line sex for salary in a house in Honolulu. A girl could make fantastic sums of money there provided she was lucky and her health didn't disintegrate under the exposure to every scabby disease known to man. She needed that money, she said, to buy a motel for her brother when he returned from service in Japan.

Years later, I met her in Nevada, wearing Levis, boots and a windbreaker. The motel just didn't happen for her. She and her brother with the Honolulu money made a pass at lady luck at the dice tables in Reno. Lady luck was busy with other passes. This left them with about five hundred dollars in their jeans. The five hundred they put as a down payment on a remote piece of land, though in time, they managed to scruff and claw their way to the development of a valuable ranch property.

"Seek and ye shall find," quoted Ruth to me as she shared a pair of highballs at the Riverside Bar.

Thelma was a poetry reader who loved dogs. She was forever bringing in a stray she'd found or rescued from the pound. "Please, Sally, just for a few days until I can find him a good home . . ." Pets, I compulsively feed and shelter, so naturally I was a pushover to this plea. Imagine! Dogs in a cathouse. She went off with a man one day who claimed to be a dog lover, too. He turned out to be more attached to her money than the dogs or Thelma. And when the money was gone, so was he. When I saw her again she was running one of those doleful little pet shops peddling tiny fish and barrels of food mixtures. It was one of those sad stores where a little bell tinkles when you open the front door. She died, a lonely suicide, in a south of Market Street hotel. I was the one person who attended her funeral.

A happier, daffier ending winds up Bernice's story. Bernice was a chubby blonde with a beautiful speaking voice. When we closed Pine Street, she disappeared.

One day a handbill arrived in my mailbox; no note, nothing more. A gospel evangelist was coming to a town far from San Francisco. This handbill went on to say that "Our Sister," together with her "Power of the Blood Choir" and "Brother Martin" who was "also a powerful speaker" had redeemed many a sinner throughout the land. They promised to redeem a few more sinners with their free-will collection. The photograph on the handbill was my Bernice; the name was different. I have wondered if the collections for her were as good as those at the Establishment. . . . Bernice had a melodious voice and a persuasive way with sinners when I knew her.

Among others who dropped by the Establishment was a medical doctor who had interested himself in my staff; he was a sort of house physician. He looked down the throats and tested out reflexes and generally satisfied himself that everyone was nice and healthy. This medico often stopped in for conversation and light refreshments.

Just after I had met Frank Egan at the Policemen's Ball, the doc and I were chatting at one of the old places of mine at 676 Geary Street. I mentioned Frank Egan, the Public Defender, who was also a conversation-bearing buddy of the doc's. They really shared a common attitude toward Captain Dullea, whose habit of breathing made them most miserable.

"It's a funny thing, Sal," said the doc, looking like he was shopping for a headache. "I love Frank and no one could tell me anything bad about him. But now, I am just wondering if he leaks a little at the mouth after a few snorts at the bar."

I asked him how could he ever come to such a conclusion.

"Well," he said, "you know how it is with my practice. Now and then I get a patient or so with a little hole in them or maybe a little old piece of lead that has to come out for health's sake. Often these patients are shy types who have no desire to increase their social circle, particularly in regard to cops and such."

"Recluses," I said. "How does Frank thicken this plot?"

"Well, I hate to even think of it," he said, "but the last two or three such types that I have discussed with Egan when he drops by my office mornings . . . the last two or three have wound up captured by the cops within twenty-four hours. It's very depressing."

I told him he could whistle that tune again and in the same key and asked if the hangout spots of these people had been mentioned on each occasion.

"That's what bothers me; yes."

"But that kind of suspicion is crazy. His job is springing not busting them."

It was not solved for many a long month and when it was solved it came the hard way. Two days later Egan got a page one top billing in connection with a first-degree murder case and he wasn't even the corpse. Mother of God! The Public Defender of San Francsico cast as the heavy and a candidate for full treatment on a number one murder rap! To many, less stir would have resulted from headlines that Saint Peter had been pinched.

The details were a little hairy.

A middle-aged woman, Jessie Scott Hughes, was found dead in a street end near her home close to the Pacific Ocean beach. A pretty good attempt had been made to make it look hit-and-run. Homicide Chief George Engler, a very smart cop, had little trouble proving she'd been done in elsewhere and laid out at the cul-de-sac street.

It looked like a real fat mystery. George Engler had more answers than a barrelful of fortune cookies. His story went like this: two of San Quentin's graduates (just recently exempt from another trip back to the alma mater thanks to Frank Egan's courtroom skill) were sought for the actual act of murder.

Mrs. Hughes had been grabbed in her own garage, slugged, and then ironed out rather thoroughly with her own car. The corpse was taken to the end of Ocean Avenue in a Lincoln sedan borrowed from a friend who was a Fire Department lieutenant.

No sooner had these thugs spilled Mrs. Hughes on her own curbstone than they took off for the Latin Quarter and stuffed themselves with a huge Italian dinner. They had worked up a hell of an appetite obviously.

Mrs. Hughes had just taken out a fifty-thousand-dollar life

insurance policy with guess who as a beneficiary? Right again. Frank Egan. The whole thing began to take on an air of a dime novel detective story, but the thing that makes it all different, regardless of how it's written, is that it is absolutely true down to the last comma.

No one likes to talk about the dearly departed, but I don't want anyone to have the opinion that Mrs. Hughes was just a simple-living old dowager who was set upon by any unscrupulous society. As a matter of fact, I happen to know she was no shrinking violet by any name. She was *truly* a wolf in friend's clothing. A she-wolf at that. She knew Frank was happily married to a charming little gal and had several young and wonderful kids that he treasured. She played up to him at every turn and dogged him wherever he might go, not to mention the fact that she was many years his senior.

In those years I didn't drink, and I drink just slightly more than that now. But I went to many a bootlegging joint, especially the one at Franklin and Ellis, where Frank used to hang out a lot, with the other city hall types. They went there or down to the old Philosophers' Inn on Merchant; ironically, it was just across the street from the morgue. It was in these two places and in many others as well that I would see sweet Mrs. Hughes three sheets to the wind, ordering more drinks and yelling at the top of her lusty lungs, "Charge it to Frank Egan." I guess she figured that if she advertised it loud enough and long enough, her relationship with the guy might become a reality.

He was forever worried that his wife would find out, but he was far too kind a man and far too considerate for human life ever to have done anything about it himself, or by using someone else.

Egan had an alibi. He had been seen with my medical friend, the house doctor, at the fights the time it was supposed to have happened.

But the police had found out too much (true or not) and much too fast. Unless they were using a little soothsaying down at headquarters, I had a hunch that something more was in the picture than most of us could see. My private guardian angel was blowing the E.S.P. trumpet full blast. I found a nickel and a phone booth and called the good doctor's office. He was in. In and wallowing in a good brood over a whole multitude of things. I asked if he and Egan had discussed the accused San Quentin graduates in his office within the past few days. He said they had. He added that the two murder lamsters had been Egan's clients.

"How about Mrs. Hughes? Was she an item, too?"

Doc wondered why I wanted this information. I told him I suspected I could clear up the mystery for him and vindicate the famous Sally Stanford intuition.

"She was another Egan client. Sure we talked about her."

Now I was 95 percent certain. I asked him to search his office thoroughly, "pay particular attention to the light fixture above the desk, around the telephone connection, especially the wiring at the terminal," the usual bugging places . . . Suddenly a word came into the phone, a word not found in the medical dictionary for the term it refers to.

"You found it?"

"I found it."

So my trustworthy extra-protective sense was right again. The police had bugged the doctor's office and this explained why the gendarmes had been able to give book, chapter and verse on the activities of the heavy-handed murderers and the other things ad infinitum.

Confirmation of all this came later when Captain Dullea was Chief of Police and told the press he'd put a tap on the doc's phone hoping to catch a few fish. He had never expected to catch as big a one as Egan though. The rest of the story was a clambake for the press and the thrill-seekers.

Egan chose to duck out for a while and get his thoughts and plan of action straightened out. He sent his wife Lorraine to retain Vincent Hallinan, the fiery left-wing Irish Lawyer who was just beginning to burn up the courts in California.

Vince Hallinan is a valuable friend to have. He has acted as my attorney many times and is one of the best scrappers in the profession. He entered the courtroom to win Egan's case with two strikes against him, an unfriendly umpire and the sun in his eyes.

I'll never forget this fiery, handsome Irishman's defense of Frank Egan. I predict that someday all trials will be on *Candid Camera* and every act and move of the judge will be bared for all the world to see. The judge in that case was Judge Frank Dunn, and I have never known a more ruthless man.

In the midst of that trial, he found young Hallinan in contempt of court and ordered him to jail. Under the laws of our land and the Constitution, you are allowed an attorney of your choice. It certainly was denied Frank Egan when the judge told Tennan, one of the other defendants, that his attorney could continue the defense of Frank Egan. I know whereof I'm speaking because I attended every day of the trial and watched Judge Dunn overrule every step of the way. I can only hope that some day, jurisprudence will record every uttered word. The higher Appellate and the United States Supreme Courts would then be able to review justice at work via motion picture and tape. Because it's only in the misconduct of the district attorney and the errors of the judge that one can receive a new trial. But jurors, at least most of them, are laymen.

"Well," they say to themselves, "the judge said it was so and the D.A. said it was so." And, of course, that impresses the hell out of most of them.

The Lady of the House

It all reminds me sometimes of the slaughterhouses in Chicago where the Judas goat runs back and forth, taking thousands of poor innocent lambs to their death because they have no mind of their own and *must* follow the leader.

In the end, the two hoodlums elected to "cooperate" as a small consideration for their lives. One bared his rancid soul of its festering secret; he said he and his partner were hired by Egan to kill Mrs. Hughes. On the basis of this testimony, Egan's conviction was obtained. Hallinan had fought such a splendid battle that the jury didn't go all the way. Just life imprisonment.

Fate dealt Egan another dirty blow a few years later. His unrelenting enemy, Charles Dullea, was appointed to the Adult Authority. In California, the Adult Authority is the parole board that annually considers applications for release from the penitentiary. One of its primary requirements is that each applicant be penitent, an attitude that requires admission of guilt. Egan, in the quarter century that followed, would never consider copping out to the murder of Mrs. Hughes. Dullea finally retired from the Adult Authority and immediately afterward, the bitter, still angry old man was paroled to a world he could hardly remember.

On the surface, that evening when I saw him again at Frankie Carter's after the long intermission, he was pretty much the same. He was "almost lifelike" as they say of a job done by a good undertaker. He remembered me, after a little coaching, and we kidded a bit and had a drink as I studied his still fine features and wondered if he really had given the death order for Mrs. Hughes. I thought not. It was far more conceivable that his two grateful and admiring clients might have thought they were doing him a favor—a favor which might mean a few bucks in their own pockets when the insurance windfall came to him.

After all, the whole thing had taken only a few minutes—less than an hour—not too much effort for them; and no expense at all.

It's just like Brigham Young always said: "Everyone wants to know which wife I slept with last night; no one cares about my true religion." People are still curious about the madam's personal love habits. Well, I did get married a few times, and it sure as hell wasn't for money.

Love is not all fire, sex and passion. Those fires flare up, go off like a sky rocket, and fall like a clinker in the bottom of a grate.

Husband Lou Rapp was handsome and charming. He was artistic and a swell man. He was also compulsively neat. He still is. I am a tidy person myself, but Lou was a cleaner-upper with a fervor! I never knew whether he had taken the brass hinges off the doors, polished them and forgotten to screw them back on firmly. Opening doors while married to him was always a gamble. One time he arranged the parlor of one of our homes with gorgeously new upholstered sofas. He was so proud of his work he got carried away. He even stretched a piece of ribbon across the front of the sofas to prevent anyone from sitting in them. It was like the de Young Museum!

Lou and I acquired property. We worked hard and were very good friends; we still are today.

Bob Gump I had known for about twenty years before we decided to run in legal double harness. For a Gump to wed Sally Stanford was rather improbable to the rest of the world. Bob is one of the sons of the prominent Gump family of San Francisco. They own the famous and very deluxe Oriental art store which always reminds me of the Metropolitan Museum with cash registers. For instance, you can pick up a pretty good bargain in an ancient Buddha for twenty-five grand plus sales tax. The store has become a status symbol in San Francisco; gifts in Gump's distinctive wrappers are very important to some. Bob Gump was something of a curio himself. Looking at it all from here, I suspect it was not the happiest moment for Bob's family to learn they had annexed me as a shiksa. But at the time it never crossed my mind.

Bill Graham in Reno gave the unblushing bride away and then we flew back to my home at 3235 Clay, where my staff at the Valhalla had prepared a wedding supper.

It turned out to be a very lively social event. The bridegroom was a little high on the bubbly. The toasts were bounteous and plentiful and poor Bob, overcome with emotion and excitement, got a little stiff. Someone set fire to the john. The firemen, irritated all to hell because the guests' parked cars blocked their access to the fire hydrants, called the cops. The police arrived and distributed tickets like confetti. The guests were furious and beefed at both the cops and the firemen as well. It was all a very gay and dizzy omen.

We separated two years later.

Bob Gump was a lovable guy, saturated or stone dry, and even if ours was an unfinished symphony, we managed to put on a performance that kept me and most of San Francisco diverted. *Life* Magazine covered the story with full-page photos of the bride and groom.

Once, when Bob was in the mood for retrospective thoughts of his childhood in San Francisco, he told me a wonderful story.

It seems his mother, Mabel Gump, had taken his brother Dick and himself aside when they were about eleven or twelve, and told them as much as she thought she could about the facts of life. When she had told all within the realm of propriety, she took her famous husband, A. L. Gump aside and said, "Abe? I want you to tell your sons about the facts of life. I've told them all I could, now you must elaborate on what I've said and discuss it with them. When you take them to synagogue this Saturday, you tell them all you think they must know." The father said he would, and that Saturday, his sons by his side, they walked down the Green Street Hill toward the synagogue.

A. L. Gump was always a proud man, the epitome of social prominence and stature. He always carried a gold-headed cane and wore a Homburg hat.

As they walked along, Bob's stately father stopped suddenly, turned toward his sons, who stopped in their tracks and looked up at their father, and A. L. Gump spoke in his deep and official voice. "Boys . . ." he said, pausing for a long second, "don't go with whores!" The stunned sons stared up at him and he said quickly, "That's all!" and they continued down the hill to the services.

One of the local columnists reported that two little old ladies were chatting as they passed by the famous Gump store in their chauffeured Continental. "Oh," said one, "there's the famous Gump's. They are getting very prominent here, aren't they?"

"Yes, yes, indeed. Why one of them recently married into the Stanford clan."

Bob's relatives could not escape the endless publicity. Some of the society editors and all of the gossip columnists took up the torch with devilish delight. Every move I made, short of a trip to the disposal, was depicted as a major social event in the life of "Mrs. Robert Livingston Gump (the former Sally You-Know-Who)."

The Gumps had been reported to have been involved with another famous lady of the night, Dodie Valencia. Dodie was one of the most famous madams before the 1906 earthquake. Mr. Gump Senior was having a rough time as a merchant. Dodie admired a painting that was for sale at $16,000 plus in the Gump store. She would have to think it over. True or not, it is said that Gump's were about to close their doors forever. Dodie heard the news and took the cash to Gump's and the painting to her house.

The Lady of the House

The Gumps and I agreed on one thing. I was not concerned with the ancestry and source of income of my clients—obviously neither were they. The point of feelings was the difference between a contract of sale and the contract of community property.

So, Bob Gump and I finally decided to run down two different roads. I flunked in patience and Bob needed a vacation. Consequently, we had a friendly divorce and lived happily ever after.

Though Bob is the oldest son of the family, it is his brother Dick who inherited the management of the store. The clerks there still call me Mrs. Gump, and Dick is always cordial. It's a nice feeling when I shop there.

Then Bob Kenna came into my life, good-looking, smooth-talking Bob K., who was the middleman in the marriage list I collected. Right now I do not know for sure who has the highest score, Barbara Hutton or me.

Kenna was strictly a ladies' man. When it looked like my bookkeeper was too close to my husband *and* my accounts, I let them both go. The bookkeeper was a pretty kid and was shocked and surprised when I told her that a devoted interest in either my bank account or my husband I could possibly condone; but not both.

To be truly successful in marriage takes a lot of attention and devotion to the cause of togetherness. Compulsively I married the cause of making money. It is a habit with me. Like many a veteran hunter I get buck fever and go after it. When you start out with less than nothing, the barren years haunt and threaten. Billionaire Paul Getty and I have a similar problem. We both hate failure in anything. We both have a few in the portfolio of marriage. It's par for the course.

Practically all of my husbands are friends of mine. Responsi-

The Lady of the House

bility to a loved one does not always end when the separation contract is signed, believe me. I still say it makes no difference *which one* was the most loved. Sometimes I loved the cause we fought for together; sometimes when the cause was gone, the feeling was gone, too.

With some, the feelings are still there. My seventh sense has always worked when I cared for a person or a project. It tells me what to do. Consequently, I believe in this thing lots of people dismiss as "hunch" and others call "a woman's foolishness." Extrasensory perception has been lauded by some scientists and poohed to nothing but coincidence by others. One ex-husband has no doubts about what mine did for him.

Intuition, promptings, warnings, psychic premonitions, call it what you will, have been a vital part of my life from my earliest recollection. Hardly a really tragic or vital change has come into my life for which I was totally unprepared. In every instance, it was announced to me by the "bonging of my special gong."

Actually what happens is an intense and urgent awareness of something about to happen to me or mine. It was as insistent as the beat of a jungle drum early the afternoon of that fateful New Year's Eve.

I had gone home to bathe, dress and relax before a late-hour celebration of New Year's Eve. You have been, I know, in a room or house supposedly completely empty. The insistence that someone is with you alerts your whole central nervous system even though you have heard nothing, seen nothing or had any tangible perception of it.

I was unmarried at this time. The name of one of my ex-husbands kept coming to my mind. It got so damned urgent that I telephoned his number. No answer. I then called Rosanna and told her about it.

"It's probably nothing, honey, you'll find him celebrating

The Lady of the House

New Year's with a babe. But if you don't satisfy yourself, you'll be miserable all evening. I know you."

It was a cold, foggy night. I bundled up in two coats, got into my car and drove out to his apartment. The foghorns were blasting out in doleful moans. The apartment was dark. I rang the bell, no answer. I peeked in the window of the garage, his car was there. I pushed the bell hard—no response.

There was something wrong here somewhere but I couldn't put my finger on it. Just a gnawing at my stomach and my mind. I waited until someone finally came out of the building and I grabbed the door before it closed and locked again. Once inside I went as fast as I could to the fifth floor where his apartment was. The door was locked. I rang the bell and listened intently for some sound from inside. After a few minutes I began to leave and as I walked down the stairs I saw the small sign MANAGER on one of the apartments on the third floor. I started to walk past it, not knowing if I should take a chance on looking like a fool or not. What the hell. If there *was* something wrong, I might be taking a worse chance by *not* investigating.

My knuckles hurt as I rapped them against the hardwood door of the manager's apartment and so I rang the bell. There was a long pause and finally a middle-aged woman opened the door and eyed me up and down.

"Yes?" she said.

"Listen," I said, "this may sound a little silly to you, but I'm the ex-wife of the man who lives in room 528. I've got to get into his apartment. I just *know* there's something wrong in there."

After three or four minutes of explanations and pleading, all she would say was, "Well, I'm sorry. I can't do anything about *that*. If you'd like me to, I'll call the owner of the apartment house and have him come down."

The Lady of the House

"Yes," I said, "I wish you would, and hurry."

The owner was a man named Wollenberg, who lived in the penthouse of the same building. After a few more minutes, he and his son came down and he asked me what was wrong. I gave him the same explanation and at first he refused, saying, "I'm sorry, madame. I have no way of letting you in there unless the tenant approves." I began to get angry and said, "Now look, I have an apartment house too and I know damn well you have a key to every apartment in this building. I *insist* that you let me in there."

"I'm sorry," said Wollenberg, "but I can't let you in *any* of my apartments without the consent of the tenants."

"Where in hell is a telephone around here?" I said, keeping down the indignation and rage as best I could. He let me use his personal phone, and for the first time in a *long* time, *I* called the police.

In a few more minutes two rookie cops, probably put on that evening to guide the New Year's Eve celebrants home, arrived at the apartment house. I gave them the same story and finally convinced them to go, with Wollenberg, into the apartment and check things out. I let out an audible sigh when they said they'd do it, and as they entered the apartment I waited outside, recognizing the fact that I was an "Ex" wife and not wanting to get tangled up in some good-intentioned lawbreaking.

After a few minutes, they came back, laughing heartily and talking to each other about, "Too much holiday cheer" and "These foolish women." I asked them if they'd found anything inside.

"Yes," laughed Wollenberg. "Your husband is fast asleep and everything is fine."

"Did you turn on the lights?" I asked. One of the rookie

policemen smiled and said, "Oh yes . . . I even flashed my light on him to make sure he was asleep."

"That does it," I said. "Now *I* want to go in there."

The group around me looked amazed and Wollenberg said, "What in the world for? We told you everything was all right."

"Listen," I said, "that husband of mine was the most annoyingly light sleeper I've ever known in my life. If you had walked around in there flashing lights in his face, he would have awakened immediately. Now, damn it, let's go *in* there."

I moved ahead of the group to the apartment, Wollenberg mumbling under his breath as he again opened the door.

Without wasting any more time, I went straight to the bedroom and turned on one of the officer's flashlights, shining it directly into the quiet figure's face. All I had to do was lift one of his eyelids and see the blank, sightless pupil that stared up at nothing, to know that something was wrong. I looked around in the bed and found several small white tablets. At the foot of the nightstand lay a little cardboard box, once full of sleeping pills, now empty.

I wheeled around at the policemen and the wide-eyed Wollenberg.

"Can't you see this man is dying?" I screamed. "For God's sake, get an ambulance and a doctor."

I don't think I've ever seen an ambulance get anywhere so fast in my life. It seemed like seconds and they were there.

Downstairs, as they took my ex-husband's dying body from the apartment house, Wollenberg said to me, "I never believed in women's intuition before. That kind of thing never existed to me. But, if I had allowed anything like this to happen, I never would have forgiven myself."

Albert Wollenberg became a superior court judge later, and after that, one of the most famous judges in our federal courts.

The Lady of the House

Many days and sleepless nights at my husband's bedside in the hospital, trying to keep hold of his mental will to live, made the nurses on the floor nervous wrecks. But I had a job to do. To bring him back. Willpower and determination did the trick and he finally pulled out of it. My job was completed, and I returned to my home and my own world again.

Eleven

PERHAPS being a charter member of the Booker T Society had something to do with my having never received the grim, moralistic treatment that my status and capers might have rated in a less imaginative and more humorless community.

I was very proud of that post.

The Booker T Society (though that wasn't exactly its name at first) was conceived, invented and swung into full action by Red Clark, the International News Service reporter on the police beat at the Hall of Justice.

The press room at the old Hall was grimmer than Edgar Allan Poe's night dreams; the ones even he couldn't bring himself to jot down. Red arrived there early one Monday morning, broke, hung over and newsless. His telephone had been left off the hook; its only response was a dull buzz. The steam boiler was doubling in brass doing an insistent but offbeat imitation of the Anvil Chorus. And there was no paper in the john.

Red told me all about it a few years later when fame and honor had come his way because of his contribution to the advancement of the spirit of man. There are occasions when all of us wonder if anything is really worth while, and this was one of those black hours for him. Red sat there glumly at the battered, scum-frosted desk that the City and County of San Francisco provided. Inspiration seized him. He picked up the *Examiner* man's phone and did a quick call to the Regal Amber Brewery. He asked for the superintendent.

"This is the press room at the Hall of Justice; when does the beer arrive?"

The superintendent tried to emerge from the fog.

"Who ordered the beer? Who's gonna pay for it?"

Clark projected shock, pain and astonishment into the phone and related his message to the unseen ear.

"Pay! This is *the press!* This is a city-wide celebration, to be attended by numbers of dignitaries, prominent citizens; maybe even your own boss. . . . Don't you know what day this is?"

The shocked silence conveyed to Red he had scored. Beer was just newly legitimatized and at that post-repeal moment no superintendent was about to horse around with any possibility of offending the press, numbers of dignitaries, not to mention his own boss. Hoarsely, he asked what day it was.

On the desk Red was using, there sat one of those calendars that know all, tell all, about the day involved. You know, like the Battle of Trafalgar, the birth of Jenny Lind, Harvest Day in Kashmir and other bits of valued information. It just happened that this was the birthday of "Booker T. Washington, pioneer Negro educator."

"This is Booker T. Washington's birthday."

"I'll be damned," said the superintendent, and after a short silence added, "By God, it *is!*" Maybe he had an educational calendar, too. "I'll send the beer right over."

Clark hung up, smiled at himself and fingered the calendar. Life could be beautiful. Gather ye roses while ye may and all that poetic philosophy spurred him on. In the next twenty minutes, using the birthday celebration of the pioneer Negro educator plus the endorsement of the Regal Brewery, he successfully and moneylessly negotiated with Max Sobel's wholesale liquor firm, the Cresta Blanca Winery, the Langendorf Bakery, and three delicatessens in the Tenderloin. Four delicatessens had actually been contacted but the telephone at the fourth had been answered by the proprietor's wife, who recognized Red's voice and immediately dunned him for the payment for a couple of pastrami sandwiches due her from a couple of Christmases back.

Naturally Red was annoyed with this. He decided to strike her off the list of participants in this splendid city-wide celebration.

He had promised dignitaries, and Red was a man of his word. He immediately called all of the out-of-work newsmen he knew, invited them and their girls; he extended cordiality to Clark creditors, including his tailor who had lately taken to muttering about a little something down on the latest set of threads. Supervisor Dewey Mead, who could make a speech at the drop of a hat, bookmaker Paul Bouquet Cohen, and Painless Parker, the millionaire chain dentist, and I arrived, along with many others who were prominent in one way or another.

The goodies and beer showed up promptly along with every son of a bitch and his brother who wasn't in jail, getting married, confined to a bed of pain or too numb to get the message. Judges, gamblers, off-duty sidewalk supervisors, cops, attorneys, county jail matrons, witnesses, recently released felony suspects, minor and major politicians and one jovial priest from Old Saint Mary's, they were all there absorbing the scene and the refreshments and asking each other blankly from time to time between mouthfuls of turkey and beer: "Where is this guy, Booker T. Washington?"

Booker T. Washington became a tradition in the newspaper world in San Francisco, and Red Clark became its high priest. As a charter member I continued to participate, and the job of special catering for this annual function became my exclusive franchise. In time the meetings became too abundantly and aggressively attended to be contained in the press room, so one of the municipal judges would adjourn and lend us his courtroom.

Newspaper editors dreaded it. No matter what safeguards they took, each year their city room staffs tended to thin out to a nothingness along about time for the party.

Notoriety brings its problems and an unexpected incident brought the need to make adjustments in the name of our jolly group. In a short time, announcements in a small paragraph would appear in each of the papers telling the initiates that the annual birthday celebration of Booker T. Washington was about to take place. And with this the word was out.

A squad of ladies arrived as representatives from the Booker T. Washington Auxiliary of one of the Negro churches. They had read about the celebration and were prepared to celebrate with us. Covered dishes, spareribs, berry pies and their minister arrived with them, and the good man of God was surprised and shocked to discover several hundred drunks present and completely unsure whether Booker T. Washington was a man, a species of dahlia, or a new way to make a martini.

Racial amity brought the necessity to adjust the name of Our Society. It became the Booker T Society, which to date offends no one.

Just a few years ago we suspended its meetings forever. Times had changed. The newer generation of newspapermen changed with them. These were sterner, less whimsical lads and were largely aloof and unamused at such obviously adolescent shenanigans.

But while the society was still alive, I had one very San Francisco thing happen to me and friends of mine. This meeting was held in the courtroom of good, mellow, old Matt Brady, who was long District Attorney of San Francisco. Matt loved to sing Irish songs and there was plenty of Irish singing there as soon as the first few kegs were cracked.

The friends of mine were very pretty girls. Matt liked pretty girls almost as much as he liked Irish songs. I told the pretties to get in on the harmony and two of them draped themselves around his shoulders all through the last verse and chorus of "Rose of Tralee." There was some squeezing going on. The girls squeezed, Matt squeezed and a fotog friend of mine from the *Examiner* squeezed. He squeezed the gadget that controlled the shutter on his camera.

The following Monday morning the first case to appear before Judge Matt was that of two young ladies charged with responding unwisely to a call at the St. Francis Hotel. As they looked demurely up at his honor, their attorney offered him—not an exhibit—but a photo of his clients. The girls thought the judge might like to have a photo souvenir of a very happy occasion.

That's right.

Case dismissed.

Romance without finance is a nuisance, but that was not our problem at Chez Stanford, for one of the great lovers of love and politics from a far eastern city got a fix on one of my debutantes. He was married, mayored, and publicized over most of the world. Women flocked to him like lemmings to the sea. But it was the Little Flower that captured his heart.

One of the Herculean tasks we all find requisite is the destruction of our innocence. When innocence is gone, much of the splendor and wonderment of life is gone. But the Little Flower kept that exciting childlike newness about her for as long as I knew her.

You have heard me say over and over that many a woman's

appeal to her man might weather the big storms of marriage were there a little more whore in her and a little less shrew. The first lesson my debutantes mastered was not the calisthenics of the mattress. These girls came on smiling. Each of them wanted to please, to listen, to charm and seduce a man's mind as well as his emotions. They were determined to please, to interest, and to create empathy rather than analyze their clients.

They played their roles without rehearsal or direction. They improvised the script to fit the need and they made the men feel important. The illusion was created and kept active that as long as he was a client, he was the most wonderful and important client in the world.

The Little Flower made every man feel as though he were the most, the greatest, and the first seducer in her life. They loved it.

Her specialty was: If you catch me you can have me. Believe me, when she got through ducking behind the draperies and playing the coy virgin, he knew he had caught the prize. She was the cutest little thing.

And the great man seriously considered risking his career and his marriage to have her for his very own. I have seen this happen more than once. I believe it was this very quality of sincerely trying to please, to adjust to the man at hand, that brought thousands of Japanese girls to wife with our servicemen. Compare this delight with the offerings of our own carping daughters, the pride of the local PTA!

The Little Flower did not wed the great political figure and change the history of an important city. She had her own plans. Mother, wife, and social leader she is now right here in Marin County.

It is true you won't get a mink hanging over the sink; it's also true a girl has to get out of bed now and then to show one off.

The Lady of the House

Some of the most important love games are played off the mattress. Professional man-pleasers go into the game as professionals. Much of their strategy is far more personal and spiritual than it is physical. The places which offer twenty minutes in bed with a girl at an exchange of a few crumpled dollar bills are not parlor houses.

So I say again, "A little more of the whore and a little less of the shrew" could very well be the adjustment that would keep more marriages heavenly. My own marriages lasted as long as there was a mutual cause to fight for and as long as the two of us could have more fun in accomplishment than either of us could manage separately. I like a clean challenge and I am compulsive about accomplishment.

Little did I dream that soon I would be involved in the most sensational courtroom drama and would receive unbelievable notoriety. Most of all, I never thought that I'd be forced by law to face charges that really had nothing to do with me. Charges of which I was completely innocent. Most assuredly I didn't expect to be accused by a person I had never seen.

All because someone very close to my mother, namely my brother Merle (second oldest of my brothers), was very foolish about a girl. There is no "I" in love; and when a man and a simple girl disappear in romantic flight from the ranch where he works, the wild accusations fell right into my lap!

The girl was the niece of the farm's owner; and Merle had gone there, after constantly coming to me for money, to work at the advice of my old and dear friend Rosanna. Rosanna had known the farm owner and had suggested that Merle go there to help him with his cows, about thirty of them, and make a living for himself. She made the arrangements and Merle left. I remember saying at the time that he might *steal* the cows, and after

I had gotten deeper into the mess that was coming, I found myself wishing he had. It would have been a lot cheaper to buy more cows, believe me.

Although Rosanna knew the girl and her father, I personally never saw her before in my life.

In September of 1939 some character from the Missing Persons Bureau and his accomplice came to my house on Bush Street. My housekeeper came upstairs and told me there were two men to see me. She also mentioned that they looked like policemen or "inspectors inspecting." That's exactly what they were. The first question they asked me was whether I knew a man named Merle.

"Yes," I said. "Why?"

"When did you see him last?" one of the men asked.

"As a matter of fact, I saw him last night. I asked you why you wanted to know."

The two civilian-dressed men looked quickly at each other and then the taller one spoke.

"He's wanted for the kidnapping of a young girl in Livingston."

Kidnapping? They had to be kidding. I had seen Merle several times before, always asking for money, and I had seen him last night for the same reason. I knew him well enough to know that if any girl went somewhere with him, it was of her own free will. Unfortunately, the girl was a minor, and, as far as the law was concerned, she didn't *know* her own will. Her farmer father, as well as her mother and aunt, had filed charges against Merle and a full-scale investigation was under way.

I answered all the questions the two men had for me and they politely said "Good day" and left.

I spent every minute I could the next two days searching every boardinghouse and hotel I could think of where they might be staying together. The money I had given Merle the night

The Lady of the House

before the inspectors arrived amounted to only five dollars and I knew he wasn't staying at the Mark Hopkins. Hoping to find him before the inspectors did and straighten this mess out, I looked absolutely everywhere. Later, I found that I had missed him by about thirty minutes at a hotel on Broadway and Columbus. I didn't find hide nor hair of either of them.

Two days after their first visit, the inspectors came back to Bush Street and brought a friend: the Chief Investigator for the District Attorney's office in Merced. Things were starting to get plenty warm. He asked the same questions and got the same answers.

I didn't have time to brush my teeth before two *more* unexpected guests arrived. This time it was the mother and aunt of the missing girl. They hadn't been with me but a few minutes before they went into great detail about how poor they were. They didn't have any luggage and I felt sorry for them, so I offered them a room at the apartment house. They accepted eagerly. I gave them a room upstairs between the concrete and the contractors. At that time I was completely remodeling the place. Their room didn't yet have a door on it, but it was better than sleeping in some bus terminal somewhere.

Naturally, we had a long conversation about the missing girl and Merle, and I told them, "These things happen every day in the big city, but I can understand your concern. In a town your size, it probably happens once in a lifetime. Don't worry."

Apparently they were less worried than I thought. When I asked them if they'd like to meet the Chief Inspector for the Missing Persons Bureau, they said no. Wanting to do *something* to help, I asked if there was *anything* they'd like to do. There was. They wanted to go to the Exposition.

Good grief, I thought, that's a hell of an attitude at a time like this. They even asked if I wanted to join them, and I said, "No, I can't think of doing something like that at a time like this."

But that didn't deter *them*. On $75 of my money (they were so poor) they went to the Exposition and apparently saw everything this side of Livingston. They returned home, had dinner and a little wine, and finally said they were "sorry" about the charges they had placed against Merle. They said, quite convincingly, that they would take the money I had given them earlier (because they were so poor), amounting to $250, and go back to the farm in Livingston. They finally started to leave, saying they would take a streetcar. It was getting quite dark outside.

I found out later that the reason they wanted to take a streetcar and not the taxi I offered them was because they had arrived in town with the D.A. and the Special Prosecutor from the County of Merced. The reason they didn't have any luggage was because they had been put up in the Californian Hotel.

But, thinking that they were simple farm folk and believing that I had convinced them to drop the charges against my brother, I didn't want them to be out on the streets of a strange city at night. I had my housekeeper drive them, in her car, to the bus terminal. As soon as they got out of the car at the depot, they took down the license number.

The next morning my housekeeper was awakened at her home by the aide to the District Attorney, the District Attorney himself, the Special Prosecutor and the whole damn bunch. She told them the truth. She knew nothing about anything and was actually shocked when she heard that Merle was accused of kidnapping. She had never seen anything irregular at the Bush Street Hotel.

Although they couldn't make any headway with *her*, the Law was firmly convinced that I had something to do with all of this. Besides, I was available and my brother wasn't.

From the housekeeper's place they went in a group to a nice guy named Quinn who was the Chief of Police of San Francisco. They wanted me arrested, and Rosanna too, for kidnapping, and white slavery. Quinn wouldn't have any part of it. He told them that they would have to get a warrant from their own county before he would make an arrest. He wasn't going to have them leave any of their debris in San Francisco for *him* to clean up. By "debris" he was referring to the false arrest charges and many other things that could happen if the whole affair wasn't handled right.

The next morning, I looked out of my bedroom window over Bush Street and saw the damnedest bunch of cops, all shapes and sizes, running all over the place. It wasn't hard for me to put two and two together. They were getting ready to make a pinch. I had gotten a call the night before from a dear friend who warned me of the rumble in Quinn's office and advised me to take a vacation. I told him that I never ran when I was guilty and I'd be damned if I'd run when I was innocent. But had I known the mess that was to come, I might not have been so damned available.

Rosanna and I were arrested on charges of being involved in a child-stealing plot with my brother. My brother was on the same warrant and they would find him soon. They took us to the county jail and I contacted my attorney, Marvin Lewis, who was told to get a writ of habeas corpus immediately. For some insane reason, instead of going to the judge I told him to, who was a decent guy, he went to the hardest and most impossible judge on the bench—Judge Jacks. He turned the writ down flatter than a pancake. Only having one crack at getting one, we were stuck for bail.

The Merced officers' telegraphic warrant set the bail for $500 apiece; but at 6 o'clock in the morning, they hustled Rosanna and me off to Livingston. By the time we were safely tucked away there, the bail had jumped to $25,000!

Through my attorney I had arranged to pick up $25,000 in

negotiable Liberty bonds from my old and valued friend and bondsman, Boyd Puccinelli. We all thought that would be plenty for Rosanna and myself, but when the authorities and the D.A. found out I had enough for at least *one* of us, the guy and his crummy cohorts stayed up all night preparing a 54-count information sheet of the craziest charges you ever heard of—everything from pandering, running a disorderly house, kidnapping, white slavery, you name it. They used that to get the courts to raise the bail to $100,000 by cash, or $200,000 by bond. The high bond was supposed to make the charges look more serious and make their case more binding.

My attorney went to the Appellate Court and we got that reduced to $20,000 cash or $40,000 by bond; which I made for myself at least, sixteen days later. These were sixteen of the most stinking days I've ever spent anywhere. It was a filthy hole, crawling with lice and filth, and the first breakfast I received was a bowl of prunes. I took the time personally to tabulate over 56 worms in that one bowl! It didn't make for developing a hearty appetite.

The only person who was able to separate the facts in the case was a wonderful guy, Judge Hal Shaeffer. They had, in the meantime, caught Merle and had him securely under wraps on the same warrant. Judge Shaeffer separated the case against my brother and the case against Rosanna and myself. Merle was charged with child stealing (a serious offense) and we were nailed with that long list of trumped-up bits of garbage devised and created by the District Attorney and his cronies.

While tinkering away my time in that stinking tank, I couldn't help but think that I knew the matron who visited us every day. Finally, just before I left, I asked her, "Excuse me. Is it possible that we've met somewhere before?"

She looked down her pointed nose and sneered. "I hardly see

how *that* is possible." But a light was shining somewhere in my head.

"Did you ever meet," I asked, "the former Coroner of Merced County . . . Keilberg?"

She looked somewhat amazed and said, "Why yes. I'm his widow." The light was on full power now.

"Then I know you very well," I said. "My former husband, Ernest Spagnoli defended your brother-in-law in Santa Rosa for the murder of his mother-in-law." The matron remembered very well now. It was the first case won under the new law of "innocent by reason of insanity," and Ernest had picked the jury that acquitted him.

Giving me the half-sympathetic, half-pitying look that most snobs reserve for what they term "fallen women," she said, "I hardly would have known you. You've changed so much."

I looked her over from head to toe, thinking of her switch from society matron to prison matron and said, "So have you, dearie. In more ways than one."

Strange how people change and suddenly want their pound of flesh when you are no longer of use to them.

But finally I had raised the money and left the jail. I took a copy of the Sheriff's bond, thinking I would sue him, regardless of what happened. All I could think of was the 56 worms in the putrid bowl of prunes. I wondered where the money for the *good* food went.

As for Mrs. Keilberg, the prison Matron, I don't know what happened to her, but the Sheriff, I understand, joined his friends and the other 56 worms in hell. A fitting place for him.

As I prepared to leave the prison, they tried once again to get my fingerprints. They had heard something about that American Quick Heating Electric Iron, but they weren't quite sure. They'd have loved to prove I had a past record. They tried like hell, but I tried harder, just about tearing the goddamn place apart. I have my former husband Ernest Spagnoli and my dear friend at the *Chronicle* to thank for helping me out of that place. They didn't get my prints either.

I made the mistake of interviewing one of the most prominent attorneys in Merced outside the Elks Club at lunchtime. Sitting in my car, he explained that it was a "terrible" case but thought he might be able to help me. My friend Rosanna was a "gone gosling" he said. She was too deeply involved with the case. He suggested that I contact an attorney friend of his in San Francisco whom he could work with (in the scenes behind the scenes). The attorney's name was Johnny Taft and he used to work for Billy Lyons the Bondsman. I had known Taft more years than I wanted to remember and the last contact I had with him was in the back seat of a sedan when I was trying so damn hard to be respectable. But in cow country, an attorney was an attorney. I went to see his friend.

When I arrived at Taft's office, I asked him if he had seen the Merced attorney lately. He said no, but that he expected to be contacted shortly. Taft didn't know it then, but I had seen his friend leave from the private exit and go down the elevator as I was arriving.

Taft went into a long dissertation about the "terrible" aspects of the case against me (as if I didn't already know them) and said that for a $25,000 retainer he might be able to save *me*, but poor Rosanna was a dead duckling. Had I been a little more desperate and a little less intelligent I might have bought the goods, but having caught him in one lie about his lawyer friend's being there, I didn't feel like gambling $25,000 that he was telling the truth *this* time.

I told him that for that kind of money I'd defend myself. I might have a fool for a client, as the old saying goes, but I'd sure as hell give them a fight. Also, any attorney who defended me would also have to defend Rosanna to win. "We're in this together," I said, "and we'll rise or fall together."

So, good friends, beware of retainers. They can retain you right out of your sanity, if you have any.

I left and went to see a man whom I had always had a great deal of admiration for; an attorney named Leo Friedman. He was a wonderful attorney.

We subpoenaed everybody, including the local PTA, the Christian Scientists, the Baptists, the Methodists, the Catholics, and the Volunteers of America; in fact, anybody that talked to each other inside or outside of the courtroom. The only ones who didn't show up were the Salvation Army.

So having about three hundred of them sitting out in the corridor on the day of the trial, I felt I had strength in numbers, at least. Under the law, we put the witnesses "under the rule," which meant that no witness could hear what the other testified; and that's a good way to catch one in a lie. You can do pretty well with that kind of tactics. I've caught a lot of liars with that same gimmick since then. Besides, they can't listen to all the spicy details.

Finally, the county clerk, who was a woman, came to me and pleaded that I let them go home. "Are you going to use all of these witnesses?" she asked. "Can't some of them go home? They are a great expense to the County, you know." I looked her square in the eye and said, "I don't give a damn about the County's expense. You don't think that bevy of barristers in there are working for nothing, do you? When *I* go home, *they* go home."

Merced was supposed to have a new courthouse built. I don't think they have ever recovered from the cost of that damn trial. I *know* they never got a new courthouse.

The Lady of the House

When the aunt and mother appeared in court, they testified that we tried to hypnotize them, locked them into their apartment and wouldn't let them go. They said they couldn't make any phone calls. Somehow, they had forgotten the trip to the Exposition on my dough (the money I gave them because they were "so poor"), the fact that all they had to do was stick their heads out of the window over Bush Street and half the city would be there, and they failed to explain how Rosanna and I managed to lock them into a room that had no door.

The case fell apart by the weight of its own stupidity, and Rosanna and I were never tried.

Unfortunately, Merle was convicted and sent to prison for from one to twenty years. The Feds had a hold on him for taking a minor across the Oregon border, and once *they* take you, they *must* try you. That I had to try to prevent by dissipating the charge against him before he was released. I was with him at the gates of San Quentin when he went in, and I was with him when he got out eighteen months later. That wasn't bad when you figure the time he *might* have spent.

Prior to his release, when it became known that he was coming up for parole—something that the folks in Merced naturally heard about—I received another visit from the aunt and the uncle of the girl. This time I was ready for them with a friend from Los Angeles named Bob Hyatt, a Special Investigator, and his tape recorder. They explained to me that they were so sorry they had lied on the stand but the D.A. had told them to. They went further and said that they had a mortgage on a ranch and another one on a house in Hayward that needed paying off. If I would help them, they said, they would not oppose my brother's parole. Their proposition was simple, or at least *they* thought so. I took the tape recording, which I still have, and played it for Judge Isaac Pacht of Los Angeles, who was on the Parole Board. My brother was paroled and the other charge waiting for him was set aside.

So, the truth *is* stranger than fiction, and I had a valuable lesson. That there are no crosses on Calvary. They are all right here. I am sure that God in His wisdom places the burdens on the shoulders of those who can carry them well.

Twelve

EVERYTHING went along fine, for a while at least, and the Merced mess had taken a place in the back of my mind. Everything seemed to be status quo. Then came that tragic day of December 7, 1941 at Pearl Harbor.

A few days after that date, America was deep in war.

With it came the rationing of food, sugar, coffee and meat. Gasoline was controlled, and most other items necessary to maintain some sort of life were being regulated. But regardless of the restrictions, most people in San Francisco did not find great changes in their lives in 1940 and 1941. Not until May of 1941, when they put one General DeWitt in charge of the Presidio. And the damage this man couldn't think of himself, his wife helped to do. I understand she was one hell of a do-gooder.

The soldiers were coming in and the boats were going out. The Merchant Seamen were being paid overtime and war-zone time (that's *more* pay). The town was a teeming mass. As soon as he took over as General of the 6th Army, DeWitt ordered all the little Japanese put in concentration camps. All their precious effects were stuffed into lousy warehouses, where what wasn't bought by the sharks was stolen by the custodians. Many of these creeps who housed and warehoused their goods sold the merchandise and belongings at a fraction of their true worth.

Then the general got around to the girls.

The venereal disease rate was high (so *he* said). We hardly ever heard about it when the town was controlled and before the "sea gulls" took over. That's the name not-so-affectionately given the girls that follow the Navy (and the Army too). With the unavailability of motels, etc., the boys got it where they could. In some cases, they got more than they paid for.

The ladies of the houses, who were strict disciplinarians when it came to the health and cleanliness of their girls, were appraised by the District Attorney and the Chief of Police that on May the 23rd, all houses must close and everyone must "cease and desist" whatever it was they were doing. Sex being one of the things the good general couldn't ration, he decided to stop it all together. Sadly, many a good house and woman were put out of business.

Included on the off-limits list were Ida on 6th Street, 526 Van Ness over the Tire Shop, 699 Golden Gate, Annie Iker, Eve on Turk, all the massage parlors (and God knows there were plenty of *those*), Clara on 4th Street, all the French and Oriental houses (of which there were an endless number) and many more.

Just a few remained opened and managed to escape the wrath, at least temporarily, of the U.S. Army. Among them were Alice on Bay Street, Mabel Malotte at 1275 Bay just up the Street, Ethel Edwards on Chestnut, Mona Regan on Green Street and Sally Stanford on Bush. There were a few other hearty souls that were holed up in some apartment house where the traffic was still heavy.

Everything went along more or less the same until a girl named Clara coveted what she thought was a going business at 929 Bush. For years she'd had a boyfriend who was a lieutenant on the police force. One night I was suddenly ordered to close my doors. The police lieutenant came to my place, told me to lock up and stay locked up until he was off that particular beat. To further make his point, he had cops swarming all over the place for a while. Every time a client showed up at the entrance he'd see the Man in Blue there. That would really scare the hell out of a guy. It makes going and coming almost impossible.

I always had another house to go to in case I had to shut down the one I was in, so I decided to make the apartment house over into something different. An apartment house. I was just making plans for its legitimate future when Clara stopped by. She assured me that she could take over where I got cut off. Always believing that half a loaf is better than none, I made the deal. And she did pretty damn well for a while too.

One night, while I was visiting the place and seeing how business was, I spotted her cop boyfriend standing outside her door, and listened to the conversation from the shadows down the hall. He must have thought she'd paid some cash for the business, because he was telling her she'd have to "hurry up and make her money back." He couldn't guarantee how long he could keep the place open.

I was always interested to see how far the tainted public servant would go and that was half the reason for my letting her take the house in the first place. Sure enough, she got the word from the higher ups to close. I was glad to see her go.

To make the apartment house legitimate meant silverware, and I supplied it with high quality knives, spoons and forks as well as dishes. My previous customers didn't come to eat with knives and forks. Just in case a former customer had to leave the place in a hurry from the back exit, we had always securely locked the kitchen door to hold back the Law. It was also kept locked up because the fire escape was off the kitchen and unexpected guests might try to slip up the escape steps and give us a surprise visit.

When we were finished redecorating the apartment house, it really was beautiful. They had real wood-burning fireplaces, French mantels, lovely baths, wall-to-wall carpets, expensive draperies and truly beautiful, and original, antique furniture throughout. Of course, all the French beds were equipped with Beauty Rest mattresses and Wamsutta sheets. All of my male clientele always slept on the best, including genuine down pillows. In short, they were lovely downtown apartments and were quickly occupied by honest Joes and businessmen.

My dear friend Rosanna was made manager of the apartments. As long as she was sober she was great. I didn't know how long she'd last, but she was a hell of a gal and I'd never find anyone else I could rely upon any more than her.

Finally we opened for business (legitimate I mean) and my first tenant was a man named Smith. (He really *was* Smith). He was the head of the Japanese Division of the OWI, the Office of War Information, in San Francisco. I figured he'd at least pay the rent and if he didn't, I'd know where to find him.

Shortly thereafter, on a Friday afternoon, I picked up my son at the military academy where he was going to school. Just for the hell of it, and because I was so terribly respectable, I thought we'd drop by the apartment house and see Rosanna. I talked to her over the phone a little earlier and thought I smelled a little alcohol (I've got a great smeller) and wanted to be sure everything was all right.

As I pulled up in front of the apartment house, I saw Rosanna talking to a bedraggled and tired-looking woman with a little boy of about six hanging on to her dress. She was crying and pleading with Rosanna about something, with Rosanna seeming to say no, and that's when I had to stick my nose and big, stupid heart into the discussion.

The woman's name was Champion. (She was beautifully named. She championed every cause but the right one.) She told me, between tears, that she and her child were homeless and had been living at the Victoria Hotel and paying ten dollars a night, with no cooking privileges, until she found a home. But now she had no money and no place to go, and an unemployed husband and child to feed. She begged me to rent an apartment to her, or help her find *something*. I took a look at her tear-moistened face and at the pretty little child that hung to her dress and figured, What the hell? I knew she'd never find a place to stay in the city at that time. There just weren't any living quarters available, not without paying an arm and a leg.

So I told her she could move into Rosanna's apartment and Rosanna could move into mine. I gave her a job for fifty dollars a month to clean up the place for me. And she turned out to be the cleaningest woman I have ever seen in my life. The halls were cleaned and polished beautifully.

About a week later I learned that she had another son whom she kept stashed somewhere because his face was badly deformed. He had fallen off a barn, so Champion said, and she couldn't bear to have him around her. I began to make arrangements with a plastic surgeon friend of mine to see if anything could be done. Although she had told me she had to wait until the now fourteen-year-old boy was fifteen, the doctor told me the operation should have been done long before and that there was no time to waste. It was my intention to pay for the bill and give the kid a decent break in life, but other developments began that threw me off the track. One of them concerned a pardon from the Governor of Oregon.

It was the most frustrating thing in my life.

The Lady of the House

I had placed a large amount of cash in escrow in the Pacific Title Insurance Company in San Francisco and was going to have it released to two attorneys I had hired who were sure they could get a pardon for me on the little stay I'd had in Salem, Oregon, as a child.

As soon as the pardon came through, they would get the cash (a little trick I highly recommend to you if you ever need it). They told me of their fantastic contacts, of their friendship with the Governor of Oregon and that state's Circuit Judge, J. Lonnigan, a powerful man in politics. They discussed in great detail their frequent trips to Washington to see the President, Franklin D. Roosevelt. My only mistake being my promise to cover their expenses during their fight, I suddenly found myself paying out huge sums of money for liquor and trips to Oregon.

I listened to more B.S. and I must have had rocks in my head to believe it. After five extensions on my money at the Pacific Title Company, and still no pardon from the Governor, I found the last extension suddenly running out.

At about that time I had the Vagabonds, a singing group, as tenants, and one of them told me of a strange little man who dropped by their apartment at 4 A.M., asking a lot of questions about his rent and wanting to see his rent receipts. Sid Goldie, the columnist for the newspapers, who was also living there, told me a similar story. I talked to Champion and asked her if she knew anything about what was going on.

"Oh no," she said. "I would tell you at once." There was a cagey look in her eye that I had learned to be careful of. Perhaps she sensed it too. She began to call me quite often, wanting to discuss the problem, which I avoided like the plague, always being sure not to say anything on my end of the phone. Then I found out that she had been negotiating with a little weasel named William R. Wheel of the O.P.A. for those of you who may not remember, the O.P.A. was created by some ass as a government bureau to regulate, among other things, the rents charged for the scarce apartments. I think the letters stood for Office for Persecuting Americans. The job was to work out scientifically the minimum amount the landlord could rent his apartments for, and then deduct 10 percent from that figure and freeze the remainder as legal rent for the premises. Charging more would bring the cops with a pinch, a guillotine or a gibbet; perhaps all three of them if Sally were the suspect.

Well, I was charging more. I was charging more because I wasn't going to let people live in crummy or badly furnished rental units and it took the difference between what the O.P.A. allowed and what I charged to make these places habitable. I also allowed for a small profit for Sally. I figured that would be the only way I could provide with tips and Cokes the lad who finally pushes my wheelchair around when the day comes.

This, of course, got the O.P.A. mad as hell at good old Sal, but I had been stalked before so I merely took extra care—like not trusting Mrs. Champion.

At that time I didn't yet own the apartment building. When I began major rebuilding and renovation, I had made arrangements with Dave Blain, the owner, to buy it if he ever decided to sell. An appointment had been made between Blain and me to meet and discuss the apartment house. I asked him to meet Mrs. Champion and tell me what he thought of her, mentioning to him that I was suspicious as hell. I had reason to be. Just that morning she had become a government witness for the O.P.A. When I called and asked her to join Dave Blain and me, she must have thought I wanted to try to convince her to keep her mouth shut.

As I was getting ready to meet her and Blain on Bush Street, my phone rang and an old friend in a position to know what was going on said, "You have an appointment at 929 Bush Street today, don't you?"

I said, "Yes, why?"

The voice spoke quietly but urgently. "For God's sake . . . don't talk in that building. The Police Department and the O.P.A. are putting little tin bugs all over the place."

"What should I do?" I asked.

"Well," the voice said, "if you happened to be at that address right now, you could probably find a place to hide for a while and see what's going on. You might even catch them in the act."

And catch them I did.

I let myself into the apartment of a friendly soul who lived there and I peeped through the Judas of the back door. Named after the peephole from which Judas betrayed Jesus, it was properly labeled. Just as I was about to change my position from outside to somewhere inside, someone let himself into the room with a passkey. It was the official bugger of the Police Department, Pete Keneally. We used to call him Peter Rabbit. He caught a glimpse of me and tried to shove open the back door. He shoved and I pushed and finally, his being some 140 pounds my better, his shoving won out. We stared at each other for a second and then I said, "Why Mr. Keneally, how nice it is to see you." I tried to appear as calm as I could.

Knowing there wasn't anything he could put his hot little hands on that he hadn't already had them on, he mumbled something about having to check all the fire escapes in the building, and asked why I had a door on the fire escape.

"Can I help it?" I said. "I can't baby-sit with the tenants and watch what they're taking on or off, doors or no doors."

There had been a pretty bad fire a few days earlier in which four people had died, but I thought Peter Rabbit was a little out of his class checking fire escapes for the Fire Department. Besides, I had spotted all the little wires running up and down the steps of the fire escape and the back stairs of the apartment house as well. As Peter Rabbit started down the steps, I couldn't resist opening up the Judas and saying after him, "Peter darling, I've heard that bad wiring can start some pretty bad fires, and this is one you won't put out so easily."

I really had the idea of waiting until they all went to lunch (something they wouldn't miss, considering it was free) and then stealing all of the goddamn equipment, about ten thousand dollars' worth. They wouldn't have been able to do a damn thing without tipping their hand, and bugging a place is illegal anyhow. But I didn't do it. Now I wish I had.

Suddenly the doorbell rang and a little wizened jerk stood at the door. He said, "I'm William R. Wheel, of the Office of Price Administration for the United States Government. These are my credentials."

I looked him right in the eye and said, "You don't have to prove it . . . you look the part."

With that, I brushed by him on the stairs, almost knocking him over, and took up a better vantage point in the lobby. There were only two ways to take out those little tin suitcases full of wires and bugs: the tradesman's entrance, which I had covered by a little tailor who lived in the lower part of my building; and the lobby door where I stood. They couldn't try to get out with the equipment without my raising holy hell.

Better yet, I stepped up to the telephone and called every major newspaper in the city, including the *Chronicle*, the *Examiner* and the *Call Bulletin*, and gave them all the exclusive facts of how my place had been bugged and the culprits were still there. And my God, the newspapermen and photographers came in droves.

I stood outside on Bush Street watching Wheel's men take their little tin suitcases out of the apartment house under the eye of the press. Wheel walked up to me, crumpling an empty pack of Lucky Strikes in his hand, and asked me for a cigarette. He apologized for what was going on and said that he was only

The Lady of the House

doing his "duty." I gave him a Pall Mall and he said, "Now, I wonder what the O.P.A. would think if they caught one of their agents taking a bribe of a pack of cigarettes."

I grabbed the pack back and shoved them into my pocket.

"Bribe? Those things are hard to get and expensive. You've heard about digging a hole too deep, Wheel?"

"Are you threatening me?" he said.

"Hell no," I said. "I'm promising you that I'm going to shove you in the hole you dug for me."

The war was on, and that made two of them.

You know how it is when thieves and jerks fall out. One blames the other. The press had a heyday with the story, and no one knew anything about anything. The regional director of the O.P.A. was George Monchard. He blamed Wheel. Wheel blamed Peter Rabbit and Peter Rabbit blamed them all, including Chief Dullea.

Everybody backed me up, even the Apartment House Association. That's one of the few organizations I've ever joined, and I'm glad I did. They not only picked up the fight, but so did all of the papers. The *Chronicle* wrote a terrific editorial called "Invasion," concerning one's private rights. The Ford Committee in Washington even took it up. By this time, William Wheel was talking to himself. He was carrying a gun with him everywhere, and had taken up drinking great quantities of rum and Coke.

My friendly voice called me again and told me that Wheel had been drinking heavily in his office one afternoon and had left a big fat letter on Monchard's desk. Everyone speculated that it was a letter of resignation. I had a bar at 1409 Market Street with a perfectly good teakettle. I asked that my contact take the letter to the bar and use the teakettle to open the flap. I had to know what was in it.

It was thirteen glorious pages long and filled with wonderful bits of scandal. I made notes of the contents and again called the *Chronicle*. It contained information that named places that had been sold, rents that had been raised instead of lowered, and people who had asked for relief and had been given far more than they'd been entitled to. Many other interesting irregularities were mentioned.

I supplied the *Chronicle* with Wheel's address and they arrived at his house as he was entering it with a case of rum and plenty of Coke. He was in a very talkative mood. What the letter didn't say, he supplied the two reporters. Not only did he say it but offered to write it out and said, "I'll sign it." Which he did. Mr. Wheel had *permanently* resigned by that time.

Somehow (I can't imagine how) the information got around that Monchard's brother was selling rotten eggs and butter to the Government for a half a million bucks. I've often wondered whoever could have told them.

In fact, I've often wondered how the O.P.A. charge happened in the first place and about the strange coincidence of Wheel's having been a process server with the same team of attorneys who were trying to get my pardon from the Governor of Oregon.

So I figured the hell with lawyers and decided to go to Oregon and see what *I* could do about cleaning that childhood blemish off my record.

I had made up my mind that I had lived for twenty-five years with that sword over my head and it was time that was ended. During my talks with the powers that were in Oregon, I found out a few interesting facts that didn't really surprise me. Judge J. Lonnigan, a supposed close friend of my attorneys and a national Exalted Ruler of the Elks from Oregon, had never heard about me *or* my case. So, through Senator Bill Strayer (whose daughter Nadine I had attended school with) and Senator Rex Ellis of Pendleton, a meeting was arranged between Governor

Earl Snell and myself. This was done without money, without booze, and without expensive hotel and travel expenses.

Snell was aghast at the story and at my youth at that time. He commented that that sort of thing "couldn't happen today" and wished he could give me back the years I had lost because of it. He said, "That I can't do, but I can give you a full and unconditional pardon"; and on August 17, 1947, he sent me that precious document, with the great gold Seal of Oregon on it.

A short time thereafter, this darling man and all of his successors were killed in a tragic plane crash out of Klamath Falls, Oregon. Just less than four months after I had gotten my pardon.

Wherever he is, and I believe in reincarnation, I hope he hurries back. I've known few men with his principles. His death was a great tragedy and a personal one to me.

Meanwhile, back at the O.P.A., I took the money out of escrow that might have gone to the two attorneys in my pardon case and hired a great little attorney named Arthur Shapro, who assured me that he had never tried a criminal case before. He was scared to death. I told him I'd rather lose with someone like him than win with a lot of other jerks I knew.

My charging more rent than the O.P.A. allowed netted me eight or nine counts of criminal contempt, and in that area you are tried by a judge without the right of having a jury. In my case, I drew a judge by the name of Paul St. Sure. When you went before *him*, you were "sure" of going some place, and it wasn't home. He was quite generous (with my time) and gave me thirty days in the county jail and a fifteen-hundred-dollar fine.

After appealing it in every court short of the U.S. Supreme Court, Arthur suggested I stop wasting my money and start serving my time. So I did. I arrived at the county jail in a calico dress I had bought for the occasion in the basement of the Emporium. Nothing is too good for the county jail.

I spent the first night on a cot in the dirtiest, filthiest jail this side of Merced. One dame in the cell with me had sores all over her body and another had elephantiasis in her feet.

The next day I sent word to Shapro about the conditions and he had me moved to a semiprivate "suite" with filthy beds and pillows so rank you had to wrap them in newspapers before you slept on them. I soon graduated to the kitchen, where I was able to "acquire" sugar now and then which I put in empty mayonnaise jars thrown out by the prison staff. I also "borrowed" cream that was used for the Matron's coffee (whenever her back was turned), which I was able to shake in a mayonnaise jar until it turned into butter.

When my thirty days were up the Matron, a portly dame named Mrs. Scott, said she was sorry I had to leave and wished I could return every day at 11 A.M. to serve their lunches. I declined the invitation, but perhaps my culinary duties there stuck in the back of my mind and came out when I finally opened the Valhalla.

I figured if I could serve those freeloaders for nothing, I could sure as hell serve them better for cash.

A jealous female can create a goddamn ruckus, too. One who had an emotional fix on a suitor of mine was inventive and, to me, completely unfunny. She had just learned that the handsome lad involved had asked me the question to which I replied, "I do." Before we could get the marriage license signed and processed, she devised her master plan to be the nauseous nuisance.

Late one night when the festivities were at full swing on Pine Street, delivery trucks from every Oriental restaurant in town arrived within a few minutes of each other. Each was jammed with cartons of hot food. Each driver claimed in various degrees of pidgin English that he was to leave all this food and collect the bill. Pine Street was jammed for blocks with delivery trucks from Chinese food houses all trying to deliver egg foo yung and shrimp fried rice!

Hardly had that been straightened out when a huge furniture van arrived filled with mattresses from a major department store which at that hour was certainly closed. The delivery lads said they had to leave the mattresses and collect the bill and that they were ordered for my 1144 Pine Street and had to be delivered at that hour by express orders of the purchaser. While we were still explaining that we had all the mattresses we needed, a huge van arrived loaded with miles of carpets and that delivery man said he was going to leave them out on the street unless I accepted them. His boss had raised hell making it clear that this order had to be delivered at night and was paying an overtime bonus for the delivery man who'd work that odd hour.

Naturally, it was too late at night to phone the store. We certainly had no use for an order of wall-to-ceiling carpeting— enough to lay a super highway from here to the Taj Mahal. So we just refused the order.

The imagination of this daffy damsel was running amuck, for just at this moment several undertakers' wagons arrived and the lads in the professional suits came up to the door with the baskets for the bodies! Well, enough of a joke is sometimes just too much and for me this was it. I set Jackson on one phone and myself on the other and going down the list in the telephone book, we called every mortuary listed and asked them had they received an order to pick up a corpse at 1144 Pine Street, and by God every one of them said yes! Some had just departed, others were just leaving, and we told them the body had already been picked up. I know you are certain which body I would have put in the first basket had I been able to put my hands on her.

With the help of the police and the places of business we trapped that bellicose babe with the prankster habits. She was the secretary of my immediate husband-to-be! And as soon as he found out who this genius of the telephone really was, that score was settled.

Other scores have to be settled in person and through the force of your own willpower. One ambitious chap decided to pay me ardent suit. As I have mentioned several times, the path to my bedroom is paved with all the legalities and the marriage license comes first with me. A number of charming and sometimes wealthy men made a bid for my affections and occasionally one would make a near score. This eager lad turned out to be as useful to me as a rubber key. But his ardent attentions had awakened my interest. We talked of marriage and he had plans. He attested to know a great deal about antique paintings and had discovered a treasure which he insisted was an unknown masterpiece. It was a huge painting and the frame became more useful to me than the canvas or the subject of the artist's labors. Latin types who are marinated in the Romance languages seem to be very large in their reaction to cupids, madonnas, and suffering saints. This painting was of a sad cupid enclosed in a huge wreath. One thing for sure, it was old.

Some guys bring flowers, chocolates, bits of jewelry to the object of their affection. This inflammable Latin tried the painting. Just as I was beginning to feel warm and tender about him, it was disclosed to me that the path of true love is seldom smooth and this path was rutted with a wife who hardly understood him at all. He would get a divorce, he said. We would experience bliss and our days and nights would be blessed. He was so ardent and appealing, I went along with his project and our hours passed together were mostly spent discussing the happiness to be. Many people believe anticipation is far more gripping then realization. To me, anticipation is the waiting period for the payoff on a long overdue investment. The divorce got stalled along the way for not having been started. I decided the moment of truth was crowding me and the showdown was the only move that would give me any satisfaction with this misunderstood lover.

It was one of those magnificent days in San Francisco. Technicolor could take an object lesson in the sheer beauty of the scenery. I decided to meet my gallant admirer and had tucked the painting in the back seat of my'Lincoln convertible. We met and I told him it was either get on immediately with the divorce or off with the marriage plans. He got a little hysterical as some Latin types do when faced with an issue involving an immediate decision.

He vowed his love for me was extravagant, large, and fervent. He also vowed that his church would not allow a divorce and he really could not give up his children.

There we were, sitting in the front seat of my Lincoln with the top down, and he was thrashing around like a puppet whose strings got caught in the Mix Master. I thought he was about to hit me. It is said that grand opera developed when two of these animated vocal types met on a street corner not far from the Vatican and a political discussion started. Before several minutes the discussion had developed of its own acceleration into a full-fledged duet.

In trying to subdue my ex-husband-to-be, a struggle developed and he fell over the back of the seat of the car and plunged his pretty curly head right through the painting of the doleful cupid. His head was exactly where the head of the cupid had been. He was dazed and slightly stupefied; he had requested that we have the privilege of showing his wife the wonderful painting. I was angry, annoyed and a little miffed by his way of handling his great love for me.

His wife and children lived just around the corner, so I delivered him to his doorstep. I dragged him still wrapped in the painting right to the door, where I took out my lipstick and wrote across the base of the wreath right under my Latin lover's chin: Cupid Comes Home.

Now that is the only time I will admit ever to framing a man. His was gold leaf, rococo and baroque, and most significant of all, it was of his own choosing. It seems fitting to me that he should have it at the parting of our paths. I am sure his wife had reason to misunderstand him. I hope that she understood him better when she opened the door to receive him gift-wrapped, for after ringing the bell I drove away to my own *palacio d'amore*, where negotiations were spelled out more simply, contracts were made, and no one seeking a little love to ease the hurt caused by a misunderstanding wife ever got framed.

What's the difference between getting a ham sandwich, a house and lot, a mink coat or some coin of the realm? There we go again. The man still trying to get something for nothing.

Thirteen

I HAD no way of knowing that the dark clouds of November, 1949, had 24-karat linings when destiny and Lady Luck pulled the plug on my career and turned my temple of love into a near mausoleum. Actually, this was the beginning of the best years of my life.

The key to the whole situation was an irresponsible teen-age tramp whom I'd never seen in my life. A series of coincidental events did the trick that Sergeant John Dyer, Chicago gangsters and do-gooders from all over had been unable to accomplish.

Let's call this unscrupulous tramp Evelyn.

The most angering part of a month-long, front-page hassle was that the immaculate forces of law and order used the phantasies of a one-dress doorway hustler to accomplish what they had not been able to bring off naturally and legitimately: The Fall of the House of Stanford.

Little Evelyn set the wheels in motion on the evening of November 6, 1949. The Establishment had just finished one of its gayest and most successful years since that marvelous tour de force of 1945 when we monopolized the social crowd and the United Nations delegates.

The Lady of the House

I was at my Clay Street home when a couple of vice squadders observed a skinny little twist in purple slacks using her makeup mirror to case a possible score. A loitering citizen was giving her the eye in the neon jungle at Turk and Taylor streets, the center of San Francisco's Tenderloin.

It was early for hustling and underneath the mascara, eye shadow, and pancake makeup, this girl was clearly a minor. So the cops trailed along. She picked up her score and they picked up her. On the way down to the Hall of Justice, Evelyn turned into the answer to a policeman's prayer. She blithely told everything she knew and then she ad-libbed.

Hustling was not her greatest talent. She had more imagination than Hans Christian Andersen, Scheherazade and Baron von Münchausen. She played her role with that guileless, wide-eyed air of injured innocence that had been popular ever since the *Perils of Pauline* had captured the imagination of callow cops. It was a plot right out of Max Sennett comedies. She had been, she said, betrayed by a wealthy lecher (whose name she couldn't remember), captured by the white slavers, sold into sexual slavery, and hustled into the fleshpots of San Francisco. The who, how, and why of these events she could not explain. She claimed she had worked for Mabel Malotte, for Dolly Fine (who hadn't been operating since long before Evelyn got out of diapers), Nell Duclos, and for Sally Stanford. She was a wow at Sally's, she said.

With an audience of policemen gathered about her, her recital became more imaginative and melodramatic. Some of the cops must have been ready to crack up as they listened to this skinny, pimply, juvenile delinquent describe her scarlet triumphs, for some of them had seen the exquisitely groomed beauties who entertained the carriage trade at my place.

These lads had exhausted every gimmick in the book trying to crash my wrought-iron gates and had failed, largely because of the relentless efforts of one woman—me! And now they figured success was theirs because of the efforts of the gabby pigeon, Evelyn. This pigeon cooed and talked and basked in the warmth of their approval and really warmed up to her story.

Now they had a minor confessing-all, pointing the finger which changed the charge from a mere misdemeanor—such as a brothel keeper, to contributing to the delinquency of a minor. Contributing is a felony which could mean the penitentiary.

The cops joined hands with the District Attorney. As soon as the Deputy D.A. saw the tramp who claimed to have earned princely fees from lewd millionaire playboys, he ordered a ban on press photographers. This situation was not one where a picture would substantiate the evidence. The poor little sparrow showed no evidence of wealth. The D.A. quickly turned her story into an affidavit, the affidavit became a series of warrants. The witch hunt was on. And I was witch number one.

I hadn't been on Pine Street, except on rare occasions, since February 5, 1947, when the two robbers, Monroe and Sitler, entered my home. Having been hit over the head twelve times with a gun, I had been in and out of the hospital many times and wasn't exactly in the mood for socializing.

I had heard about this little dame being arrested about thirty days before the actual raid on Pine Street and I had heard what she said. But after thorough investigation, I was certain that she had never been through the iron gates of 1144. Her testimony during the trial bore that out.

From a highly bleached blonde with mascaraed eyelashes and penciled eyebrows and a beauty mark on her chin (which she called a "tattoo"), she was transformed by the D.A.'s office into a typical schoolgirl type with flat-heeled Mary Jane shoes and a demure little blouse and skirt. I remember asking my dear friend Boyd Puccinelli at the time how old he thought she looked and he said, "Thirty at *least*."

The Lady of the House

All this happened during an election year and sometimes deputies get visions of grandeur.

On November 6, 1949, I received a call sometime around midnight at my private number from Jackson, my majordomo, who was at Pine Street watching the store. We had a code for trouble and I knew what it was he was trying to say. Remembering Merced and knowing a little more now about being "too damn available," I figured I'd give the authorities a little time to separate the wheat from the chaff before they talked to *me*. I called a newspaper friend of mine who lived in Tiburon. He suggested that I stand outside of Alma Spreckel's house and he'd pick me up right away. "If the cops are looking for you," he said, "they won't expect to find you there."

I waited in front of her beautiful mansion, with her rococo and fairyland pillars that support the façade of her fantastic home, and my friend soon picked me up as he'd promised. We went to his home.

My attorney, who was out of town, finally returned and we talked the thing out. Pine Street had been raided and Jackson was arrested. It was a hell of a mess.

It all happened as my newspaper friend and attorney said it would. There were prosecutions, endless publicity and finally dismissals. But it was very clear to me that if I continued, I'd be on borrowed time. So I closed and locked the wrought-iron gates on Pine Street. To hell with it! There were too many squares walking the streets of the old town. Too many Johns got their jollies by making anonymous phone calls to Sutter 1-2020. I had made a decision, and I had the money to carry it through. Let prosperity get its ashes hauled out the best way it could. I was ready to go.

I had also made a promise to myself and Governor Snell that I would get out of the business. I had bought a piece of property in Sausalito in June of 1948 and I had made up my mind that on

The Lady of the House

New Year's Eve I would close down forever. You never learn a thing until you're through with it; and when you are through with it, it leaves you. The raid only speeded it up a bit.

There was a lot of unnecessary sweat from the playboys down the Peninsula, and my bookkeeping system created a few smiles. It looked like a fantastic shopping list. The cops who grabbed it at the raid were dismayed to discover it failed to put the finger on anyone. For we used the names of the most elegant stores to indicate customers: Shreves, a famous jewelry establishment, might stand for Shirley; and two dozen turnips meant that Tom had purchased her services. Magnin's, followed by twelve garlic buds, indicated that George had been marketing Mary's produce. City of Paris might be amazed that radishes, lettuce, and pastrami after their name indicated that Pauline had dispensed her wares to Rudolph, Leonard and Paul. Yes, we protected our clients.

While the police were there and all the confusion of the raid was going on, one of the debutantes, who had gone on a call and been tricked into taking money from a policeman—which is high evidence in any trial—sauntered into the place with her date; and as soon as he saw his superiors there, he turned on the girl and said, "Now we've got you, too. All the money I gave you is marked."

This twist was neither the brightest nor the most charming of the lot. She was forever giving me a bad time, always asking for more than her 5o percent and sometimes claiming she had not been paid the full amount when she met her John away from the house. I had long been planning to replace her.

Faced with the fact that the marked money would surely convict her, she grabbed it from her brassiere and proceeded to swallow it. Later she called me and asked for the best method to recover it.

"Well," I said, "it's a small enough price to stay off the police records. Since you're always wanting a bigger percentage, I suggest you keep my share of this score and try a little Ex-Lax."

I knew what I wanted to be: I wanted to be an ex-madam. But the lesson of venturing into other businesses had been driven home to me: A dress shop, a candy business and some bars convinced me I should stick to my last and make a better shoe. The only things that succeeded for me were those I managed myself. I had always wanted a smart restaurant and had been dispensing fine wine and food to my clients for a long time. And somehow, now that the Establishment had been invaded by the raiding squad, I was disenchanted with the memory-filled house on Pine Street.

A few minutes across the Golden Gate Bridge, strung along the hillsides of a beautiful cove, is a little town called Sausalito. It hangs over the water like the pleasant picturesque scenes from the French Riviera. At the end of a dead-end street, hanging over a huge pier with a view of the Bay and San Francisco, was a barnlike building with a tattered sign VALHALLA. It looked good to me so I bought it. This would be my new house, a new Sally's. Now I was in the restaurant business, determined to repeat the success I had serving that other basic appetite. To me there really wasn't much difference.

Food has the dubious advantage of being legitimate, and one's customers somehow manage to live longer without sex than food, if you call that living.

Like me, Valhalla had a bit of a past—colorful, dramatic, and at times not quite legitimate. The early settlers claimed it had originally been built by a sea captain for some Russian refugees of the revolution, and when that venture closed, it served as a landing depot for liquor smuggled in through the fog during Prohibition. Pretty Boy Floyd, Dillinger's pal, had hidden out there during his West Coast tour while G-men searched San

Francisco. No one thought of looking for Floyd within spitting distance of Alcatraz, the G-men's stronghold. When I first stood in the dusty, musty room listening to the tide slap the planks under my feet, I decided this was legitimate Sally's new home.

Sausalito was a swell place to sleep when I first arrived there. The minority group who ran it kept it that way because that was their principal use for the town. These people worked in San Francisco, socialized wherever their expensive automobiles took them, and slept in Sausalito. Their point of view had defeated William Randolph Hearst. Some of them are still trying to defeat me.

Hearst envisioned a castle on the hillsides, and Sausalito might well have been San Simeon. The attitude of the landed gentry toward his lifelong friend Marion Davies caused Hearst to halt all building he had started, saying he would never finish the castle and would instead leave the great foundations as a monument to the bigotry, snobbery, and narrow-mindedness of Sausalito's hill dwellers.

So he took his money, his fairy princess and built the castle of his dreams on another cove. Hearst left. I am still here. The hill dwellers had their own clique, strange logic, and owned the land. They were the patrons of the town, the purchasers and the hirers. But I initiated a change. I was doing some hiring and purchasing of my own. This made the people on The Hill furious, but delighted a whole helluva lot of other people who did all of their living in Sausalito, wanted to do a little business there, have a little fun at a bar or a restaurant, enjoy the full advantages of a complete town.

The mere fact that I was there with a bright, interesting, new restaurant labeled "Sally Stanford's Valhalla" was bad enough. I got the rap for changing the face of Sausalito right from the first. I hardly got the carpets down and the wallpaper up before the rumble started. When the wind blew in the right direction, I could almost hear the good ladies of The Hill clacking and chittering. One dame threatened all the males of her family if they ever dared enter my place. Another woman, whose husband's entrance to another of my places was welcomed for nearly ten years, had her attorney comb the town and county ordinances to make sure there was no way to expel me before I really arrived. Another gathered about her a small clique of anti-Stanfordites and publicly announced that she was just aghast at the possibility of Sally Stanford trying to join the women's club. She needn't have worried. I have been a charter member of "the Other Women's club" for too many years.

Sausalito is divided into three parts: the Banana Belt, the Waterfront, which runs the full length of the town, and Hurricane Gulch. The Waterfront houses the largest collection of houseboat and converted watercraft dwellers, each of them a rugged individualist. In fact, practically everyone in Sausalito is an individualist, even the hill dwellers. We probably have the most colorful population for our size, and I believe we're better for it. Sausalito attracts characters. Our beatniks are deluxe, and wash all the way down to their necklines. We boast a large colony of "gay" citizens. Our bars are rated according to the degree of heterosexuality. Our artists run from inspired to lousy. Writers and sun bums punctuate the scenery. The boat people in nautical garb spice the mixture along with several thousand newcomers who prefer commuting to San Francisco to living there.

I decided the restaurant should be a real conversation maker, and I did it in Victorian and post-Victorian décor. The only modern thing in the place is the kitchen, and that is truly newer than tomorrow. The rest of the building had to be reconditioned. I found this out from the very beginning.

I had purchased a huge antique safe in Vallejo and had just

moved it into the main hall of the restaurant. Preferring to pay as I went, I had in it a large sum of cash. The workers had hardly left and I was walking around, deciding where certain bric-a-brac would go, when without warning the safe crashed through the floor and settled in the ooze at the bottom of the Bay. All my cash money in an unopened safe, and the tide coming in. Even today those who were there with me say the expression on my face was the damnedest wildest they had ever seen as I peered down that huge hole in the middle of my floor.

It took a few days to rig up a derrick and grapple the thing out of the water; and as it was carefully set down on firmer soil, I was not amused at the two starfish, the few barnacles, and the amorous leopard shark that came up with it. I got it open and was very pleased to find my cash safe and dry.

In time, the whole building was completely rebuilt. The public loved the décor. One item that always captures conversation is the famous piece of plumbing that Queen Marie of Roumania carried with her on all her travels. It was installed and removed from hotels, private railway cars and homes wherever she stayed, and for a throne, it's a handsome piece of porcelain, glazed and decorated with loving care.

No one occupies it now. It is retired from active duty and sits in regal splendor, doubling as a planter for exotic greenery. The grillwork between the bar and the main dining room consists actually of ornate, highly polished brass bedsteads retired from service. And the little heart-shaped leaves of philodendron twine lovingly around the designs that have witnessed the heart-felt passions of many a happy couple. Candlelight, Tiffany glass shades, chandeliers and fresh flowers arranged in magnificent chamber pots keep the guests amused while the kitchen staff prepares food in the finest San Francisco tradition. It is a place to remember.

There was but one flaw, one gnawing dissatisfaction. My

name still was not on the license for the bar. Valhalla was mine except for control of the main artery of any good café—the bar. I had to do something about that.

Nobody expects to be blackmailed until it happens, and then it seems so unreal that you want to laugh at the blackmailer—it always sounds so much like a slice out of a bad late, late movie.

Valhalla was just beginning to catch on, and I was not about to discourage its success, when one evening a beetle-browed and glowering character with padded shoulders and Tenderloin haberdashery was announced to me by the obvious bodyguard who accompanied him as Jimmy Tarantino. I knew about Tarantino. He operated a scandal sheet that had gained a foul reputation for shaking people whose circumstances made them vulnerable.

Should you have a shady past or a delicate present, should you be running for office, should your citizenship be cloudy, or should you be struggling to pull your business out of receivership, you were Tarantino's cup of tea. There were two choices open to you: One was to put an advertisement in his *Hollywood Night Life*, a scabby periodical that was circulated at irregular intervals throughout California; the other choice was to throw Tarantino out on the asphalt. For this you received free advertising in the magazine itself. Your story might be phrased in ignorance, in unpunctuated sentences, but the message would be loud and clear. Should you go the tribute route, the price of the ads were on an impromptu sliding scale that was geared to the size of your fear and gullibility. In my case the threatened exposé was old hat; and when I didn't immediately jump to the opportunity of buying an ad, Tarantino blasted me on his radio twenty-three times and advertised me in his paper though I had never okayed the bill.

I first met Tarantino at a lunch that was given for the man-of-the-month. The tossup that particular month was between Judge Twain Michaelson and Jimmy Tarantino. Judge Michaelson was the man-of-the-month. I was working night and day to get the liquor license at Valhalla in my own name; and of course, being called every kind of snake in the pit publicly in print, and on the air, was doing small stuff to convince the Board of Equalization that I was sweet, rehabilitated, legitimate, square Sally. Tarantino's accomplice went by the name of Jimmy Jones, and between them they were scaring money out of locked closets and into their own greasy little hands from one end of the state to the other. The blasting they were giving me fell into the hands of the San Francisco District Attorney's office. They had taped conversations between Tarantino, Jimmy Jones, and others as they planned their attack and strategies, and my name had come up in these discussions several times. At the same time Judge Michaelson and others were convinced that I ran a clean place and I should have my license in my own name; and they felt that getting Tarantino off my back would help convince the Board of Equalization.

I didn't know until much later that Tarantino and Jimmy Jones were taping the crummy dialogue they called conversation when they talked with me. I called them blackmailers, told them to do their worst, and I hoped for the best. At the man-of-the-month luncheon I had given a check for five hundred dollars which was supposed to go to the Shriners' Hospital for Crippled Children. I caught onto the melody when I was told to make it out to Tarantino. I wonder if the hospital ever saw the check.

A man named Hal Lipsett, who had a tremendous business as a private investigator and was considered to be a trusted friend, came to me and told me that Tarantino had a tape of me calling him a blackmailer. According to Lipsett, they had said they had Sally "over a barrel" and I got more than suspicious. As I listened to the tapes from the District Attorney's office months later, the wool flew off my eyes when I heard my old private-eye friend's voice cooperating in the maneuver to shake me down and relieve me of Valhalla. The boys with the blackmail journal were listening to a tape of me calling Tarantino and Jones blackmailers, and they were being taped by the District Attorney's office unbeknown to them, and at that point my long-time and trusted friend cried out in his unmistakable accent, "You've got her; she's yours! Now, you've got Valhalla!"

I was in good company though, for Tarantino attacked a schoolteacher and hung the red banner of Communist over her. She was brilliantly defended by Attorney Gardner Johnson. The Grand Jury closed the magazine and the bully boys went to San Quentin.

It is said the easiest person to con is a con-man, that a salesman is a pushover for a new sales pitch, and I understand that during his hearings with the Grand Jury, Mr. Tarantino received anonymous messages promising to expose those creaking skeletons from the closets of the members of the Grand Jury. Apparently he believed the information would come through.

In my brushes with the Law, it hadn't occurred to me to attempt to shake down the judge or the jury, but I am grateful that Tarantino, the blabbermouth, assisted me getting my own name on my own liquor license for my own café. It was the nicest thing that happened in 1952.

We drew everything but nuns and nudes on opening night, and I knew we were a success. Everybody arrived. Well-wishers, evil wishers, delighted friends, envious enemies, natives from down the street, and some who'd come all the way from Los Angeles and Seattle for the opening. There were morbid curiosity seekers, San Francisco police brass, true food fans, celebrity collectors, and celebrities—middle-size I suppose. There were press agents hoping for the business, and politicans hoping for no tabs—both got a drink on Sally and my best wishes for a long and happy life. I no longer needed their services.

Ex-husband Ernest Spagnoli and his nice wife arrived; ex-husband Lou Rapp brought his fears that I'd go broke and jump off the bridge; Jake Ehrlich and lobbyist Artie Samish arrived, columnist Herb Caen, and a few hundred others whom I knew and loved, with even a few people from The Hill. We even had culture well represented with the presence of the able general manager of the San Francisco Opera Association, Paul Posz, and his wife Marian.

I got the license, but this was only the beginning of a feud with the liquor control authorities that at times promised to be endless. A number of years afterward, in 1955, the control of the sale of alcoholic beverage passed from a state agency called the Board of Equalization to a newly formed unit referred to as A.B.C., Alcoholic Beverage Control. This change placed me in the hands of a gentleman—Frank Fullenwider, the area liquor administrator in the new agency.

Mr. Fullenwider went to work on me immediately. He acted as if he had been looking forward to the job as one of his nicest projects. In the next five years he did his level best to kill my license. I assumed that his idea of a task well accomplished would be to take Valhalla away from me and shift me back to running a "Men's Club" for tired husbands. (Tired of what they had!)

"A woman of her reputation and character should not be in the liquor business," was his official statement on the matter. I'm sure he will always remember me; I fought like a tigress.

I learned a little more about the courage and consistency of the average square citizen at this point. During the hearings that followed, the officials who had granted me my license three years before were summoned to testify. Despite the fact that they delivered the license to me in person at that time, now they not only failed to remember granting the license, they couldn't even *place* me. They had never seen me before in their lives. Of course, on the other hand, they were being asked to remember me at a moment that was very embarrassing to them.

The only exception in this situation was the head of the Board of Equalization in Mill Valley, Gus Phillips, who had placed my name on the Valhalla Liquor License in 1952. He was then, and still is, a fine man, one who always did his job fairly, and who stood up to Fullenwider in opposition to the testimony of his own associates.

And during these first hearings I learned something about attorneys. Very few of them are worth their weight in subpoenas. The first attorney I had hired to present my case prepared my defense so badly, leaving out several points of evidence and potential witnesses in my favor, that when we lost the first hearing and then attempted to appeal the case in front of the Alcoholic Beverage Control Board two years later, the appeal was denied.

My first lucky break in many moons came to me in the form of another San Francisco attorney by the name of Richard Gladstein. From the time I lost that first appeal until today, almost ten years later, he has remained my attorney. The first thing he did was attempt to repair the damage done by the first attorney I had by filing a Writ of Mandate in the Courts of Marin County in hopes of reopening my case. This failed too, but not before the presiding Judge, B. V. Curler of Susanville, made the comment: "Had I been the trial tribunal I would never have made such a judgment. But, the record in this case was not protected and so there are no grounds left for appeal here."

But, thankfully, Dick Gladstein was not disheartened and he managed, amazingly, to keep my case alive, and keep my business open, through paperwork and appeals, for the next three years. He kept me in business until California had a new Governor, Pat Brown, and the ABC had a new State Liquor Director, who was ordered by the Governor to straighten the matter out. It was reported in several papers that the tough, but fair, new Governor thought I ran a first-class restaurant; that I had completely rehabilitated myself, and that he could not, in good conscience, oppose the continuation of the license. During his new State Liquor Director's investigation there was suddenly no reason for anyone to forget anything embarrassing.

One witness surprised me with his claim that I was "a Pillar of Sausalito's Society." I got my license for keeps. In my book Pat Brown is a man of courage, style, and class. In memory of Fullenwider's determination to stop my license, I had delivered to him a beautiful statue of Quan Uin, the Chinese Goddess of Mercy. It was returned to me with a virtuous note to the effect that as a public servant he could not accept a present. I replied, "It isn't a present, dear; it's a possible source of therapy."

It's hard for small minds to believe that a sinner can come clean. All kinds of jolly Joes insisted they knew what went on upstairs at Sally's Valhalla. One evening the Sheriff and four frozen-faced county commissioners strode into the place and said they'd heard there was "action" to be had upstairs. They grimaced knowingly when they got to the word "upstairs." It's the same grimace these boys on the town use when they're talking about anything that can be spelled with four letters, if you know what I mean.

I greeted them and admitted there was some action available there. They asked if I had any objection to their going up right now—before anybody could be warned, they added cleverly. I sighed and admitted that I had no way to stop them. I warned them not to be shocked. They'd probably encounter a naked body as soon as they got to the top of the stairs.

They did.

Just beyond the door at the top of the stairs was the naked body, as advertised. Three-year-old Richard, the son of my food checker, always managed to work his way out of his pajamas within half an hour of being put to bed. He was fast asleep and greeted them face down in the pillow, bottom up.

And one of The Hill ladies managed a *nuit d'amour* in my upstairs too. This antique doll had very strong ideas about me. She had been one of the prominent agitators to keep Sally out of dear Sausalito. She was a soft, fat, bulbous collection of oozy cells wrapped around a nasty-tempered cash register which she used for a brain. Early one morning while I was preparing for the G.O., after the last customer left, I noticed a light flashing from the upstairs window. Usually I would have been fast asleep in my San Francisco home, but something had kept me there. Looking around, I found a ladder propped against the side wall of the building. I climbed the ladder and peeked through the window and there she was, the vitriolic, fat-assed matron from The Hill, with a handsome muscular young man in tow, probing through furniture and looking into drawers of old desks and bureaus stored up there. I watched for a while and learned they were looking for money. But then they found a pile of mattresses in a corner and their minds turned from money pleasure to another kind of fun, and lo and behold, right there under my eyes, they proceeded to carry on as though they were privileged guests at 1144 Pine.

Well, if it had been anybody else, I would have laughed it off. But she had been so unpleasant and so determined to run me out of town for being that kind of woman. That made me mad. So I scurried down the ladder and removed it from the side of the building and called the Fire Department.

Before the fire laddies arrived, the young man discovered the ladder was gone, but he found a flimsier one in the attic which he lowered to the side of the building. I was watching him from a vantage spot in the parking lot. He then tried to help his fat playgirl out of the building. She was too fat for him to hold in mid-air. The ladder wobbled and swayed, and she shrieked, so he pushed her back through the window; and when he crawled in after her, I removed that ladder, too.

With the help of the Fire Department she got out. And I faced her with a not-so-gentle reminder that there was no charge for the use of my place. That one was on the house. If she returned to her hill dwelling, I haven't seen much of her since.

The john is a strange place to find high adventure, but it was in my john that Harry Bridges, head of the International Longshoreman's Union and the only honest one I've ever met, found it. I'll bet when he heads for a john again, he'll make damn sure the trip is necessary.

Harry was at the Valhalla on a mission of mercy. He was talking to two ladies, one of whom had recently lost her husband, a member of Harry's Union, and he was trying to cheer her up and help out in any way he could. Harry, the distressed wife, and her girl friend, who had originally called him, had come to the Valhalla for a few drinks after having dinner downtown. Harry never drank, but as the ladies drank Alexanders and he sipped at a ginger ale, he decided to go to the men's room.

I happened to be in the cocktail lounge at the time watching the cash register, some waitresses being overambitious coin collectors who try to become independently wealthy in one night.

As soon as Harry entered the place, which wasn't planned for boxing, two men who had been waiting for him began to belt him with everything but the commode. A few other characters had taken up residence in the place and immediately a tremendous uproar broke out.

The noise from the john hit me from across the room and I vaulted a little old lady from Petaluma (whom I haven't seen since) and charged into the place. It was like commencement day at the funny farm.

Harry was slugging away better than any Golden Glove entry. He was doing well defending himself against both goons. Some poor citizen, obviously out of training, had interrupted whatever he was doing at the trough and tried to quell the storm. That turned out to be a mistake; he was getting a pretty good quelling himself. His glasses had just hit the floor as I entered. I figured the stuff on the end of his nose was not catsup.

The single booth had an occupant; a short, fat man was trying to get out, though whether to help or to escape was not clear. He was handicapped with his trousers around his ankles. When he saw me, he modestly canceled all departure plans and backed into the booth like an alarmed gopher.

I joined the activities at once. I grabbed one of the goons by the back of his coat and, to my surprise, whirled him away from Bridges without much trouble. Then I went to work on the other character. This was a mistake because Goon No. One immediately tried to frame me. He grabbed a painting from the wall and applied it to my head full force. The frame didn't fit me very well, and the only damage done was to the painting, a good likeness of Pinhead McCarthy, a former San Francisco politician.

Meanwhile the mediator from the urinal was pawing around the floor trying to find his glasses. With the other hand he held his nose. Harry was still boxing Goon No. Two. The poor fat guy in the booth opened and closed the booth door. Goon One tried to kick me in the groin and missed. Unfortunately Henry, my maître d'hôtel, joined the maelstrom at that point and Goon One's kick connected.

The tide of the battle was turned and suddenly one of the Goons made it to the door and was gone. By the time the rest of us had disentangled ourselves and followed him to the foyer, he'd disappeared from the restaurant. The local police could not find him, but his partner was pinned to the floor by Henry. The cause of the attack was no mystery to Harry Bridges. There had been some dissension among the unions and certain elements were out to get the labor leader, but with muscle.

For a short, unpleasant while afterward, I wondered how soon they'd get around to taking care of me. The next day I received a bouquet containing thirteen daisies, plus an anonymous letter. The letter said I'd be dead before eleven o'clock. It failed to mention what day. This happened quite a while back, so they must have had a pretty long-range plan in mind. (Or maybe they lost my address.)

And then the Governor from Texas joined us in full ranch regalia, high heels and all, sporting what must have been a 30-gallon white hat. After dinner I showed him through the place and we stepped out on the boardwalk, where, as on any waterfront, occasionally a stiff breeze comes up. Without warning his beautiful hat flew from his head and settled on the tide like a white sea gull in the moonlight. The tide went out, the hat with it. The Governor was dismayed. A crowd of people gathered from the café to watch. A frolicsome wave brought the hat almost to the shore and we rushed in a band to capture it, but just as we arrived, out to sea it went again. This went on a few more times and it became a contest for the Governor's hat. Quite suddenly a small boat appeared, and a charming man dressed as a fisherman rowed alongside the hat and picked it out of the water. We all cheered. At last the Governor would have his property back. But no, the seaman bowed graciously, placed the hat on his own head, and rowed away into the mists of the night.

Maybe it was the roast duck but I like to think it was Sally Stanford who pulled the people into Valhalla in droves. I'm probably right. After all, there is nothing like staring at someone you regard as a greater sinner than yourself to stir up the appetite and create an interest in heady wines. We began to see everyone, but *everyone*. Society people and squares from Salt Lake City and Pawtucket, junketing Congressmen in town to investigate vice, and the vice types they were investigating, movie actors and international financiers complete with dolls. The scene was punctuated with ordinary butchers, bakers and even a few candlestick makers; one Candlestick Park maker was Charles Harney, the millionaire contractor who built San Francisco's baseball stadium for the National League champs, the Giants—I had them all.

A formidable battalion of my clientele was composed of wives strongly suspicious that the heads of their households might possibly have dropped in at 1144 Pine Street back in the old days. At Valhalla that kind of dame became as standard as the plunging neckline and tight pants are to Harry Belafonte's show. I could spot them the minute they came through the door. Toward the end of their meal they mumble something about freshening up their makeup and then head for the place to which women, after they have reached a certain age, refer as "the Little Girls' Room." On the way to the toilet the lady will tap me, tell me she's always wanted to meet me, ask me to have a drink with her, I always go for the okeydoke. The lyrics may be a bore but the music being played on the cash register always comes sweetly to my ears. Craftily, with martini-made shrewdness, she arrives at the subject of friend hubby; and when she roguishly puts The Question and points out hubby, I always say I have never had the honor of his patronage. She believes me not one damned bit. Way down at the bottom in some primeval layer of her femininity, she'd hate to think that hubby lacked the masculinity to try a little outside quiff for a change.

Which reminds me of a neat reply I got from a remark that I made to Mrs. Lawrence Tibbett, wife of the opera singer, when we were introduced. "I've never had the pleasure of meeting your husband," I said.

"I'm so relieved," she sweetly replied, and I knew just what she meant.

Most of the ladies of the polite world are convinced I have the answers to a lot of other questions. Most of their queries are about sex. I find that most women—even women who are traveled and sophisticated and knowledgeable in all the usual areas—are incredibly naïve.

These women are stubbornly if vaguely convinced that professional lovemakers know about unusual techniques or special gimmicks that are a few light years beyond anything that takes place with homemade love. They feel sure they can turn their males into panting, glassy-eyed love slaves by learning these trade secrets.

A sadder woman is she who feels her husband is slipping away from her; some have already been deserted. These poor dames desperately wonder what they did wrong in bed or didn't do right; maybe it isn't too late. For all these insecure sisters I try to put it on the line: No man can be held throughout the day by what happens throughout the night. Headshrinkers and Freudian therapists may give contrary advice, but while they have the theory, I had the laboratory. I'd really like to have some wonderful sex secret to offer them. Sometimes I feel prompted to make something up. It might even work. Frustrated dames will buy anything in the hope of post-menopausal pregnancy dangers. A certain Baron von Salza is in court right now for relieving wealthy grandmothers of a few thousand dollars apiece, promising them overactive ovaries through the use of raw eggs and massage. Every woman knows a little massage does no harm. So perhaps if the mattress were wired for Muzak and . . .

There is an endless line of beautiful girls, some clever girls, even well-married girls, whose problems are non-financial, who want advice on turning themselves out. They think they'd like to sell it. I tell them all to stay out of the business. The good reasons have nothing to do with morality. I figure morality is a private and personal matter, and if a gal is going to go the goodness route, she is not going to do it for goodness' sake.

There is too much amateur competition today. The professionals have learned how to run a profitable thing without managers and madams. The whole business is cluttered up with scabs and it's hardly worth the hassle.

Even the scabs, though, come around brain picking. Their usual concern is the oldest female fear I know: "Should I continue to give him what he wants? Will I lose him if I stop?" To this silly dame I have only one response: Romance without finance is a nuisance. Few men value free merchandise. Let the chippies fall where they may.

The food, décor and service at Valhalla are probably the best in the West. Gourmets of the world have told me that. But the ladies come mostly to see "that woman" and I love it. Many have a preconception of a madam that comes out of the late, late movie on television. They hope to see a Mae West with a gravelly voice, one who cracks her knuckles to attract attention to the rocks on her fingers and uses latex for makeup. These people are perpetually amazed when they encounter me. Well, I don't crack my knuckles. They explain their shock with "Actually, Miss Stanford, I expected to see some tall, old, lantern-jawed, bleached blonde." And others say "Is she still alive?" and look astounded when they find out that I am.

Frequently a guest arrives who is spectacularly noticeable. There was one who weighed around 250 pounds and steamed into my salon as a luxury liner might come into port. She wore a stunning, huge hat piled with outsized roses and violets, the rest of her upholstered in regal brocade that set someone back a fair piece of change. Appliquéd to her shoulders was a crossed fox cape competing with a collection of sparkling rocks on her fingers, wrists, and bosom that would have bailed out a brace of bank robbers. She made a big entrance; she was strictly impressive.

A covey of lady customers calmly approached and thanked her for a wonderful dinner and delightful evening. Several called her Miss Stanford. She didn't straighten them out. She accepted their thanks and invited them to come again. My flamboyant friend was delighted and delightful; she's a plenty social dame and the heiress to a steel fortune. A bit later two of the erring ladies returned and discovered that *I* was Sally Stanford. They were miffed and so was I, for reasons I don't clearly understand.

One memorable evening, a gentleman high in the ranks of the Alcoholic Beverage Control Board came to the Valhalla for dinner with his wife. Sometime during the evening, after they had eaten dinner at my expense, this little lady of his scaffled one of my best chafing dishes (or tried to) by shoving it deep into the recesses of her girdle and heading for the door.

Luckily, she was so stiff that she tripped as she slipped out the front door and fell on her face, the chafing dish clattering out of her girdle and onto the deck. As they say, "I stood there amazed, and asked as I gazed; does their glory exceed that of mine?" That was taken from "Home on the Range" and at that moment I wish I had been back on mine.

A few months later I had the privilege of seeing this same gal's husband testify against me at the ABC Board trial. He didn't know me at all. But I knew that he was wondering how much, were I to take the stand, I would tell. I declined the honor of "talking" to him.

I put 1144 Pine Street on the market, but getting that establishment accustomed to respectability wasn't an easy chore. Like some old bag that's acquired a taste for racy living and is reluctant to return to quieter things, that old house was hard to convert to just plain housing. The public was always eager to go through it on the pretext of giving it consideration. Everybody wanted to test the beds.

For a while a church group dickered for the lovely old place, and I encouraged this deal because it struck me as a charming idea. I informed them that the collections had always been good there, but they finally took a powder on me when someone took the head person aside and spelled out to him the current meaning of the term "riding academy." Apparently, he had confused "horses" with some similar word.

I rented the place to a female who said she was the former Lady Vera Dall-Beryl. She planned on opening an antique shop. Her opening bash to announce her business and create goodwill prompted the offering of the premises to the Stanford Convalescent Home Guild. This is not one of *my* projects. The other Stanford, the University, runs this caper. She felt 1144 was just the spot for their annual benefit, and the benefit very nearly went to the post. Then someone blew the whistle on poor old 1144. The affair was hurriedly canceled. Lady Vera was mortified to tears, although she had been surprised at the number of late calls she'd had from perfect strangers. She hadn't the remotest idea that 1144 Pine Street was anything more than a nice, old house (which is something like claiming to have subleased Buckingham Palace under the impression that it was formerly a comfort station). Lady Vera and I terminated our relationship rather abruptly. She wasn't getting privacy, I wasn't getting my rent, so the lights went out again.

I leased the poor old place as a restaurant. They called it The Fallen Angel. The restaurant failed. I finally sold it to a wonderful old friend of mine who said he bought it for nostalgic reasons. I understand it has been resold and is to be replaced by a modern condominium.

The house, however, was easier to unload than my reputation. There are still people who utterly refuse to believe that Sally can't and won't rustle up a dame as soon as they convince her they're "all right."

Fourteen

A DIFFERENT kind of dame gets a different kind of fame. Of course, I didn't go around with a Bible under my arm or attempt to join the good ladies who were knitting socks for the Korean orphans. I do get behind the Little League Baseball Team with substantial support. I do attend town council meetings regularly, and I have become so civic-minded that I joined the Chamber of Commerce and became so hooked on that caper that I became first vice-president. *That* would have shaken poor John Dyer if he could have lived to know it. As a matter of fact, a few years ago it would have shaken *me*.

I rounded up instruments for the high school band; I donated ground for a playground; and, believe it or not, I was asked and gave speeches before Rotary Club luncheons. I made the domestic scene, and the San Francisco newspapers kept me in the papers with a new kind of publicity.

I can't keep track of it all myself. Sausalito and I are in the papers every other day or so. Somehow for me respectability brought no privacy. I bought a 1,200-pound steer which had just won first prize at the Grand National Livestock Exposition; and when I learned the fee his daddy got for stud services, I thought Sally had been cheated in all the years of the love business. I immediately renamed this massive animal Sergeant Dyer. He was a lot of bull. The papers referred to "legendary Sally Stanford."

I was asked to participate in "a monster benefit" to raise funds for a civic mutual project. My co-stars were Miss Phyllis Diller, movie star Richard Boone, the Jazzabelles' Barbershop Quartet, a monkey named Gigolo, an impersonator of famous females, T. C. Jones, an elephant named Linda, a lamb and two dogs. My billing was under the Jazzabelles but ahead of the monkey, and there was not even the slightest reference to anything but good, clean fun. My public image took a helluva move upward.

But every now and then some newspaper or magazine writer decides to turn a barb for me into a buck for himself and snidely refers to the inability of lady leopards to change their spots. I was written up cornily and untruthfully in the scandal sheet, *U.S. Confidential.* I sued. I shook them out and got action. I'd do it again.

On the whole, I've received a fair shake from the gentlemen of the press. I know that. I also know that the old red light may be slowly fading out of my past, but that rosy glow makes Sally Stanford good copy. I'd rate about as much interest as a Skid Row bum at a bankers' convention had I spent my life as the homespun proprietor of Aunt Sally's Goodie Kitchen.

It was the town's council meetings and my new public image that conned me into running for public office. Two places were open on the Sausalito city Council. I decided to make a play for the "Madame Councilman" label to replace madam, a fair exchange.

Most of my loyal friends were aghast at the kookiness of an ex-madam running for public office, especially in a narrow community obviously divided against itself. This election comes in the spring, and when spring waxes in Sausalito, all the wild flowers burst forth. And believe me, there are *some* damn wild flowers on Sausalito's hillsides. We have a fine collection of Double-Dealing Daisies, Snap-at-Sally Dragons, and Hot-Eyed Susans. My announcement to run for public office appeared to be a rich fertilizer for these potent posies, who were determined to defeat me at the polls. All my sensible friends said, "Don't do it, Sally." There would be new enemies to make, free meals to serve, a lot of money to spend, and a lot of sleep to lose.

It was now crystal clear to me that I had no other alternative but run to win.

I cased my opponents with considerable interest and no concern for my chances. One candidate was a builder named Russel Papenhausen. He was a fine guy who had done a lot for the community. Unfortunately, this town doesn't usually vote for those who did a lot for the town. They seem to prefer the characters that came into town from nowhere, stayed around a few months, and then ran for office with the support of the Hill clique.

One character, a former mayor who finally resigned to take a better position in Washington, D. C., reminded me of the story of Peter and Paul. As you know, Paul talked about Peter and Peter talked about Paul, but the more Paul talked about Peter, the more you learned about Paul. This jerk held down a job in San Francisco and slept in Sausalito, but he attended cocktail parties, smiled at the right people, and ass-pinched in the true tradition of most politicians. He didn't necessarily confine that hobby to cocktail parties, either.

John Gallas, a school librarian, had far less sex appeal than I did. There was an artist named Serge Trubach, and two attorneys, Hugh Lawrence and John Micou. Their mutual knock was that their law practices were in San Francisco. They visited Sausalito after dark to sleep. The remaining opponent was a shipping executive, Jan Dyk. In my book he shaped up fine as a fully qualified private citizen, nothing more. He certainly did not get to me as a municipal statesman of a caliber needed to deal with the burning issues at hand.

I felt pretty good about my chances.

The issues that I incorporated into my campaign platform were twofold: More money for the Police Department and a free public comfort station for the town. Despite the fact some of my opponents circulated a rumor that my campaign slogan was "a chicken for every cot," I promoted enough pay for cops —which is a thing about which I have strong feelings. The cops in Sausalito are a long-suffering set of people, traditionally underpaid and overworked. A well-paid cop does his job better and doesn't have to let his mind wander into areas of dropping in on gamblers, after-hours operators, and, oh yes, madams, to make up the difference in order to pay the doctor bills for his children or the rent for his old mother. In my book the gendarmes had something coming. Win or lose, I was going to get it for them. Naturally, I figured no one lost votes putting dough in someone else's pockets.

And as for the comfort station, well, the opposition regarded this as a very undignified plank. I figured that every woman who ever teetered helplessly between fury and agony as she searched desperately for a toilet that wasn't there would pause thoughtfully when she came to my name on the election ballot.

I even figured out just the spot for it. In the very middle of Sausalito's Civic Center, a focal point of local confusion, there is a strange little chamber pot of a house that serves no purpose whatsoever. The natives call it a "gazebo." It was originally designated as a bus stand. Obviously the buses didn't care for it. They all stopped elsewhere. The minute I saw it, I said to myself, "Gazebo, you're a natural-born john."

The second aim of my campaign was to turn that silly, unemployed gazebo into a temple of comfort.

The Lady of the House

The other candidates came up with the usual corny campaign
pledges: more businesslike administration, civic economy, im-
proved sewage disposal, and the like. But I stood up for my little
pair of down-to-earth causes and a small accumulation of projects that developed as the campaign progressed.

And so we were off in a shower of abuse, acclamation, sar-
casm, indignation and miscellaneous comments, and the day I
threw my hat in the circle, half the town stopped speaking to
the other half. It turned out to be The Hill against the barbarians.

My constituents were labeled mainly barbarians. They
weren't just the sun-bums and beatniks, either. They consisted
of those hardworking people who had long been without a
voice on the City Council. In fact, some of my sponsors were
the most prominent people in the community, including an ex-
mayor, a highly respected doctor and many others. Many of my
supporters even came from The Hill itself. They had the hardest time of all not bending under the pressure that was applied
all around them. So, with the residents of the houseboats along
our shoreline, the middle-class residents below the hill and a
portion of the hill above, it appeared as though I might have a
fair chance of winning.

I went the whole route: campaign managers, posters with my
name on them large enough to cause an epidemic of Spanish
spasm among the residents of The Hill, telephone solicitors,
matchbooks with me grinning sweetly with statesmanlike dignity from the covers, and a campaign headquarters at an old
Main Street landmark which used to be Ernie's Waterfront Café.

At headquarters we put up valanced curtains and upholstered
Louis XIV antiques and Persian rugs and love seats and punch,
and a beautiful girl receptionist. Some uncouth soul wandered in
the first day we opened up and said, after looking around and
casing my receptionist, "Man, sure looks like a French whore-

house." He was wrong of course. The French don't serve punch.

I was underway with my big campaign and the prospects looked pretty rosy to me. The newspapers were gentle and handled the story without reference to the past.

One San Francisco paper referred to me as "prim Sally" and chatted cozily about the punch and the cookies at the headquarters. I figured that if I stuck to the issues I wouldn't get stuck with non-issues from the past.

I was a dope.

The wild flowers on The Hill, the "tweedy people" (in the words of one of the newspaper writers), began to stir their caldrons of pitch and gather their brick bats. A lady described as an "indignant Sausalito housewife" was the first to sound the tocsin. Her complaint was that a former employer of prostitutes was seeking a position where she could make decisions affecting the local children. She announced that if the men were going to stay in hiding, it would fall on the housewives and mothers to block Sally's election! Sally! Not even Madam Sally. I would never have thought of referring to her as Susan.

"Just because Sally owns a restaurant and thrives on tourist trade is no reason why the rest of Sausalito should wish to be overrun by fifty thousand weekend barbarians."

I knew just how Madame LaFarge felt when the tumbrels rolled up with a new batch.

"These people [the tourists]," she continued, "block the streets with their vulgar, chrome-plated automobiles. They spit on the sidewalk. They gape at us natives and call us a bunch of beatniks. They strew trash in the park and generally offend us with their boorish manner.

"It is perfectly obvious that Sally exploits this human ant chain, and I deeply suspect she would like, if elected, to turn Sausalito into another Fisherman's Wharf. [San Francisco's

The Lady of the House

Fisherman's Wharf being obnoxious to some for its Coney Island atmosphere these days.] The one issue ex-Madam Sally harps on—public rest rooms—would be no issue at all if the tourists stayed home."

This housewife's suggestion was that the tourists and I could be stopped if the police would only barricade the roads into Sausalito from Friday to Monday, which is like cutting off your toe so you won't get corns.

The press called on a local twist while she was basking in the noonday sun. After announcing her measurements (36–20–35), and rolling over on her back to light a cigarette, this babe expressed grave concern that I would turn our beloved City Hall into a three-ring circus.

As spring waxed wilder some genteel souls tossed all caution to the wind and announced these remarks which baffled me:

"If you run a plus and minus column on each candidate, anyone could draw conclusions that should guide his thinking." I guess you solve that one with square root. The women's clubs preferred not to be quoted, although the rumors were that it would be the women of Sausalito that would block me. And one businessman announced a vote for Sally could only result in chaotic, riotous and bitter council meetings. And he was right, come to think of it. As long as some of the do-nothings continued on the Council with me present at the meetings, a riot was forever imminent.

But the blow that stung me was a charge leveled at me by one of my political opponents. I was accused by this virtuoso of pot and palette of having dishonestly acquired the irritating plank in my platform—the comfort-project station.

"Sally stole that issue from me," he insisted. He claimed he first got into the free-john crusade as a result of encountering a squirming and unrelieved Scotsman on the Bridgeway one evening, too late for any of the usual places of recourse to be open and not late enough to be unnoticed. A likely story. I decided to ignore it.

There were well-wishers, too:

Hillary Belloc, bearded son of the famed British author, was one of these. He put himself in my corner by announcing that if Sally could run a carriage trade bordello, she could run Sausalito. There are a great many points of similarity.

Jericho Miller, the charming and intelligent proprietor of Gas House Works No. 2 Coffee House, plunged into the campaign on my behalf with gusto: "I'd like to be able to stand up in the City Council meetings and say 'Madam Councilman.'"

And strange as it may seem, many of my supporters were intrigued to find themselves involved in a campaign where the most discussed issue was a toilet. I suppose these people had been propagandized to lend support to abstract projects which made a candidate seem important. But my gazebo could be seen by everyone every time they passed through the town. There is nothing abstract or remote about the fact that when you've got to go, you damn well have to go. Try to match a proposition like that with appeal to support civil service reform or a crackdown on speeders. At least, that is what I told myself, and I continued to bear down on the Stanfordian Doctrine of Free Urination for the Masses (S.D.F.U.M.).

I researched out the available information on the subject and talked it up before every meeting I addressed.

"Where can all these people go?" I asked my listeners. "The Hill folk can run up the hill to their homes if they are caught short. The flatlanders are not only caught short, they are caught out in the open. There is hardly a bush to hide behind."

Then I told my constituents of an elaboration on my plan: a network of comfort stations centering around the gazebo—a boon to johnless Sausalito. I called them "cadgets" and commissioned an artist, a Miss Enid Foster, who had vivid memories of

The Lady of the House

latrines she had seen in Paris in 1910. She designed an adaptation to fit local conditions patterned after the open-air *pissoirs* that are traditional to Paris streets. She put her heart into it. The result was a little dandy, a real swinger.

Lots of people, you see, were sick and tired of the slumber parties that were passing as council meetings. And they figured that all hands in the club would get some mental exercise as soon as I got my membership card. I figured likewise. Everything seemed very good, very promising, not only to me but to my friends. I received endorsement from many unexpected places. I decided to attack the Council with the gazebo at the first meeting, with the police pay raise at the second meeting, and with a few thickheads at the third. I had to come home with the prize.

Up on The Hill, now, all of the witches were polishing their broomsticks. The word was out to get Sally at any cost. The nuclear bomb might fall, the Russians could unleash murder and rape on the countryside, the Mafia could turn their children into dope fiends. None of these could compare to the immediate menace.

Meetings were held, telephone squads were put to work, doorbells were rung from waterfront to hilltop in this dramatic battle against Sin, meaning me. Curiously, I had a full report on all this jazz from one of the good ladies themselves.

Life is very funny. One of the most popular, social and "in" of the women, a member of one of the better clubs of The Hill Society, is an all-time good friend of mine—a former madam. We'd been together through all kinds of problems and many a time saved each other from a raid by passing the word along.

My friend, I'll call her Mimi, left the business some years ago. She's a most attractive woman and an asset to any women's club. She married a man of means and settled in Sausalito.

Mimi had been a member of one of the first war councils

assembled when it was rumored that "that woman" was going to run for office. She had tried to soothe their fears on this occasion, but these ladies weren't buying any balm. They were in a lynching mood.

Mimi phoned me. In fact, she phoned every night of the campaign and told me about the latest moves, the meetings held, the strategies that were worked out to bury me, the pressures—some of them pretty raunchy—that were being applied to persuade other people to fight the Good Fight and put "that awful woman" in her place. Mimi was very helpful.

Meanwhile, we were coming down the stretch, and I had quickened the pace of my campaign quite a bit. The polite approach was over. I took off the gloves. I ran half-page advertisements in the local press signed by my campaign chairman telling the voters that a vote for me was "a vote to end the City Council's outlandish follies." The reporters from San Francisco contacted me immediately. My replies were printed verbatim.

I pointed out that the City Hall was a circus. "You've got the Mayor in there playing ring master and cracking his whip for the greatest collection of clowns since Barnum and Bailey."

This got me action. The clowns took off their putty noses and fright wigs and put on their war paint. Everyone stopped attacking each other and concentrated on me. The indignant housewife who sounded the alarm against me at the outbreak of the campaign got into the act again. She was still beating the drum to underscore her concern about her young. She objected to an ex-madam sitting on the City Council and deciding "what's good for my children." I answered her in a well-reported statement:

"It is quite proper that housewives and mothers be very concerned about their children. Honest concern with the welfare of children must be supported by the realities of life. One of the big realities is that I have done more for years for the young people of Sausalito than many others can claim, including our worried citizen."

Silence from her.

Another citizen announced that electing me to the Council made about as much sense as appointing Elizabeth Taylor Ambassador to the Vatican. Personally, I think that Miss Taylor might have a very interesting time at the Vatican, but I didn't think this was the most diplomatic reply to make at the moment.

Each day cleverly derisive articles appeared in the press. There was no question that they were doing my campaign no good. In spades, doubled. The information presented was never untrue. It was souped up by the headlines and captions that turned what seemed to be whimsical stories into honeyed diatribes. I was never just Sally, for instance. I was "mink-clad Sally," or "diamond-studded Sally." I never spoke: I "chirped," or I "snapped." The Bridgeway Center was my "garish political headquarters" and my posters were "scarlet political signs." As I conversed I "twirled a huge diamond on my finger," and then— a typical characterization—"Sally's watchful eyes rotate tirelessly from cash register to talking parrot to chef to cash register; nothing escapes her."

Election Day found me as nervous as a bride who is fully aware that the wedding bells may not ring. I had confidence in me, my campaign and my friends. My election workers had come through like the Marines. The San Francisco *Examiner*, and the *News-Call Bulletin* had given me a square shake. My constituents in the Banana Belt and Hurricane Gulch had called or buttonholed every conceivable voter that remained uncaptured by the Hill Dwellers. My story was told. My charges had been well aired. I figured my odds were good. I'd have given six-two- and even that I would wind up in second place at least, which would lock up one of the two Council jobs for the little gal from the other side of the tracks.

Early in the day for a dame whose business closes long after 2 A.M., I was up and into a most gay victory dress I'd been saving for the occasion. I pinned some white orchids to my shoulder, draped my fisher furs over my arm, and Rolls Royced it to campaign headquarters. Talbot Kendell from Pebble Beach furnished five beautiful Rolls Royces, all with chauffeurs in specially made hats and coats designed after those worn by the drivers of Queen Mary in England. Everyone was there: campaign crew, townspeople, reporters, friends and staff from Valhalla, and a whole lot of friends from San Francisco who wanted to be with me at the finish. We got off to a suspenseful start.

I was told that the vote was heavier than ever before; everyone had some feeling about the issue this Election Day. At least, I'd done that for the town.

Along about noon, Mimi called me. She said the dolls on The Hill hadn't worked themselves into such a foment since Pearl Harbor. They were dragging out and voting every bedridden aunt, bewildered servant, dotaged grandfather and litter case available. "Frenzied and frightened is the only word to describe it," she said. "But don't discount it. They're all votes."

I didn't. I knew damn well it's hard to beat City Hall. By midafternoon it was clear that the contest had developed into a three-person battle; the fight was between Micou, Dyk and Sally Stanford. The rest of the candidates were pretty much out of the picture.

It was late when the results were complete enough to tell the story.

I'd lost. Dyk, The Hill's premier candidate, was first to the wire; Micou, the other Hill candidate, was second. I was one hundred and thirty votes behind, in third place. The witches had won.

Two hundred votes behind me, in fourth place, was Attorney Hugh Lawrence. The others were strictly nowhere. The artist who claimed I lifted the comfort station issue from him scored a meager eighty-one votes. I ordered drinks around for everyone and got ready for the newspaper boys, who were beginning to move in on me.

I gave them the usual people-have-spoken bit and indicated no one at the City Council need grieve over my absence there. I'll be there at City Hall, I said, right down in front, and in good voice, at every meeting.

One of them had a question: "What about your 1964 campaign, Sally?"

I winked at him.

"It just started, honey, with that question and this statement. Sinners never give up."

The *Examiner* used the final four words as the lead for their coverage of the election. The metropolitan press gave more coverage than it did to far more important political contests of city- and state-wide interests. It also reported that one of my successful opponents, Brother Micou, had a clever and gallant statement for the reporters:

"I congratulate the voters," he said, "for saving Sausalito from a fate worse than death."

I am also told that a lady present said, "Don't light any fireworks yet, dearie; one hundred and thirty votes isn't a helluva margin."

Or maybe she wasn't really a lady if she was in my corner.

In 1964, the performance repeated itself, with a few variations on the theme.

I had as my campaign manager an aggressive young public

relations man named Dick Christian who was also editor of the town's only newspaper (a weekly). This time we would have no ballyhoo, no elaborate campaign headquarters, no Rolls Royces, and as little controversy as possible. We would fight on the issues at hand, fight cleanly and win squarely. In principle, the whole new approach made great sense. *I* was for it all the way, but that little voice in the back of my head kept trying to tell me something. What it was trying to say, we found out later, was that a "clean" campaign is only successful when it's used on *all* sides. However, there were certain factions on The Hill that had other ideas. They were absolutely desperate. They couldn't say anything that hadn't already been said about my past and they had nothing to say about my present that wouldn't *help* me, so they had to extend themselves a little further.

Secret meetings were held and their plan of attack was laid. We had them confused because they expected some spectacular last-minute move out of us. We were constantly gaining supporters and voters on the basis of the issues at hand. People were tired of slipshod, almost dictatorial government.

There were only three candidates that were a threat to me: Carl Gabrielson, an incumbent; Mel Wax, a reporter for the *Chronicle*; and the wife of another *Chronicle* reporter, Eleanor O'Hara Chapin. All three were backed by the Hill forces and two of them were naturally supported by the *Chronicle*.

"Never underestimate the enemy," it is said, but I'm afraid that's exactly what we did.

A young lady who was working on my campaign vigorously, and whom I had met for the first time in my life a few weeks earlier, suddenly had a phone call from "persons unknown" at her home. Her sixteen-year-old daughter answered the phone and was asked, "Isn't it true that your mother used to work for Sally Stanford?"

Merchants who placed my signs in their windows on the main

street were called by social bigwigs and told they would be "economically boycotted" unless the signs were removed at once. One silly twist on The Hill, who was supposed to have some intelligence, walked from store to store downtown and canceled her accounts.

Bumper stickers were torn off cars and opposition stickers placed over them, but the crowning piece of political pressure was the mailing of a letter, several days before the election, to all of the voters. It was from a group who called themselves Sausalito Citizens Council, and they took phrases out of context from speeches I had made and printed them as destructively as they could against me. The group, controlled by the same powers-that-be that have run Sausalito for years, was supposed to be nonpolitical, but The Hill was desperate. Nothing mattered now, not even their own pride. They had to do their worst, and they did.

So once again I lost. This time, as my campaign manager correctly pointed out, I placed a little bit ahead of the winners even in losing. Not once during the campaign did we fight dirty, and God knows there's plenty I could have done. We lost a clean fight and that's a whole lot better than winning with their techniques.

There'll be another time and another election, and you can bet your life that I'll be right in there pitching. Next time I may not be so polite. I'm learning more about politics all the time, but I've got to learn not to say those "embarrassing things," as the press put it. One thing I said that I sincerely meant, whether it hurt my campaign or not: "I've known every crook from Maine to Spain." They played hell out of that, of course, but I meant every word, and if all the dirty linen were brought out from the homes on The Hill and laid on our main street, it would take all the "do" in Duz to clean up the mess.

Epilogue

OF all my favorite newsmen, the one I'll remember longest and best is the man whose name I'll never know. He's the anonymous gentleman who wrote my obituary for the San Francisco *Chronicle*. One of my favorite reporters, who used to do a lot of reclining of one sort or another at 1144 Pine, told me in the middle of a conversation about death that an obituary on each and every well-known San Franciscan was written and on file in his newspaper. It was even set in type, ready to slide into the chases the minute the subject slid into his or her coffin. I was fascinated with this news and more fascinated when I learned there was one on me. This was really success. Did I want to see it? I sure did. He'd get it for me sometime.

Because we always closed on Mother's Day and Easter, I was home alone having myself a couple of solo old-fashioneds in my upstairs bedroom when the front doorbell rang.

After the attempt on my life by Monroe and Sitler, I was always a little reluctant to answer doorbells when alone. I stayed put. But curiosity overcame me a little later, and I went downstairs and peeped through the Judas hole. No one—just dripping fog and silence and a brown envelope sticking out of the mailbox. I carefully opened the door and snatched the envelope. On it was typed *Obit of Sally Stanford*, and clipped to it was a slip of paper signed by my newspaper friend under this message:

> For Christ's sake, don't die until I get this back to the paper, or I'll be dead, too, or unemployed, which is worse.

Upstairs with the envelope and a newly sweetened old-fashioned, I curled up on my own bed with my own obituary. It read:

> Sally Stanford, the undisputed queen of San Francisco night life, died yesterday. Of the many madams operating in San Francisco during her heydey, Sally's girls were the prettiest and the most elegantly gowned, the place the most sumptuous, her patrons the most select. She was the friend and confidante of many of the most important figures in the life of the city.

I wanted to cry. It was like Huckleberry Finn attending his own funeral and enjoying it in a miserable sort of way. I felt so pleasantly melancholy about the whole damn thing that the tears welled up and spilled down my face.

> Warm and friendly in her personal life, she was a shrewd businesswoman who was the equal of any man in any sort of a duel of wits. Another of Sally's characteristics was her interest in homeless animals. She rescued many from the pound and on several occasions gathered up injured animals on the street and took them to a veterinarian. She often was hurt in her relationships with human beings; she said she liked animals because their loyalty was beyond question. Sally was known to her intimates as a woman of impulsive charity. She would read of the death of a homeless man, for instance, and anonymously pay for his funeral. She would send money in unmarked envelopes to disaster victims whose stories stirred her.

Someone was sobbing in the room, and I discovered it was I. I just couldn't read it any further. Perhaps I'd built too large an old-fashioned. A drink for the late, great Sally Stanford! Tears as big as bunions were rolling down my cheeks, and I realized the kindness of these words. It was the saddest obituary I'd ever read in my life. And I was thoroughly miserable as I thought how lousy it was that this poor woman had to die far too early in her life, whenever it happened.

What in hell was the use of a woman putting up with persecution and poisoned arrows for bringing elegance and good taste to a business usually conducted in dismal red-lighted dumps? In my house by the side of the road I had tried to be a friend to man. And the nicest thing written about me was destined to be published when I was too horizontal to appreciate it.

It was just too damn much.